RUTH M. BATHAUER

PARENT CARE

A GUIDE TO HELP ADULT CHILDREN PROVIDE CARE AND SUPPORT FOR THEIR AGING PARENTS

Ideas and suggestions for:

♦Encouraging parents to remain active and involved.

♦Finding the best living situation for your parent.

♦Dealing with the maze of extended care and finances.

Regal Books
A Division of Gospel Light
Ventura, California, U.S.A.

Published by Regal Books
A Division of GL Publications
Ventura, CA 93006
Printed in U.S.A.

Library of Congress Cataloging-in-Publication Data.
Bathauer, Ruth M.
   Parent care : a guide to help adult children provide care and support for their aging parents / Ruth M. Bathauer
      p.   cm.
   ISBN 0-8307-1371-9
   1. Parents, Aged–Care–United States.   2. Adult children–United States–Psychology.   I. Title.
   HV1461.B37   1990
   362.6'0973–dc20
                                                              90-34506
                                                                 CIP

1 2 3 4 5 6 7 8 9 10 11 12 13 14 15 /X2.12/BC/ 95 94 93 92 91 90

Rights for publishing this book in other languages are contracted by Gospel Literature International (GLINT) foundation. GLINT also provides technical help for the adaptation, translation, and publishing of Bible study resources and books in scores of languages worldwide. For further information, contact GLINT, Post Office Box 488, Rosemead, California, 91770, U.S.A., or the publisher.

Dedication

To Mom and Dad

- who introduced me to the Savior and taught me to walk in His ways;
- who encouraged me to do my best work and to strive to become what He called me to be;
- who demonstrated how to honor your parents by their concern for my grandparents.

Contents

Acknowledgments

John Donne, the fifteenth-century English poet and clergyman, said, "No man is an island, entire of itself; every man is a...part of the main." I was reminded of that truism as I wrote this book and thought of the many people who contributed to its contents.

I am deeply grateful to the many adult children from various walks of life who were so willing to talk with me about an issue close to our hearts—caring for elderly parents who need special assistance. Although names and places have been changed for privacy, I am appreciative of their honesty as they told of happy as well as some very painful experiences.

I am especially grateful for the professional guidance I received from Dr. Judith Alexandre, director of the B.F.C. Counseling Center, Ventura, California, who gave so generously of her time to answer many questions. No questions were considered too trite or ridiculous.

My special thanks to Mrs. Mimi A. Simson, gerontologist and sociologist, who spent hours reading my manuscript. Thanks for the invaluable suggestions, which came from years of working with senior citizens.

Acknowledgments

To those adult children who are laboring under a busy daily schedule and are caught in the added responsibility of caring for parents—this book was written for you.

Introduction

Do you remember your first roller coaster ride when you were a child? Remember those thrills, dips and chills? I do. Along with the excitement there was also fear—fear that everyone quickly and bravely denied! You knew the ride would be scary but when your "car" had slowly chugged up to that first towering peak you didn't expect to be up quite that high. Then came the first plunge that took away your breath and left your tummy in your throat. After your stomach settled back to its proper place in your anatomy you found yourself gripping the handrail in front of you more firmly, gearing up for the next breath-taking plunge.

Some years ago I felt that I was on an emotional roller coaster when my eighty-three-year-old mother was scheduled for surgery. The only thrills were the times when she showed a little improvement. The dips and chills were times of fear as her condition deteriorated.

The first emotional dip came in the doctor's office when our family physician informed my mother of her need for surgery. The chilling feeling came later when Dr. Cooper[1] privately but frankly told me the chance of her surviving surgery was very small.

"But," said Dr. Cooper, "she can't go through another attack like the one she just had and survive."

We had no choice—it was a catch-22. If we refused to subject her to surgery my mother's life was in danger, but if she had surgery she might nor survive. When my mind began to grasp what the doctor said, I was plunged into breathless fear as though the "roller coaster" had suddenly plunged into a very dark tunnel. Then, like a tiny ray of light, the words "As thy days, so shall thy strength be"[2] flashed into my mind. They were words from a Bible verse that I had learned as a child in Sunday School.

God faithfully fulfilled the promise of those words. I drew on that strength as my mother entered the hospital and as we waited for what seemed to us to be endless hours while she was in surgery. Fortunately, the day that Bible verse penetrated my fears and worries I did not know what lay ahead. I did not know that my "day" for which I needed strength from Him would stretch out into not just a week, but eight years, while Mom was in a convalescent hospital.

My mother came through surgery quite well, but then for a month she teetered on the brink of death in an acute care hospital. Several times during that month Mom seemed to improve ever so slightly. Each time she did I asked Dr. Cooper about looking for a convalescent hospital. He always discouraged the idea.

Then came another frightening dip on my emotional roller coaster. While I was seated at Mom's bedside in the hospital one Saturday morning, Dr. Cooper came in on his rounds. After examining my mother and chatting with her, he cheerfully announced, "You'll be leaving us soon."

Turning to me he said, "You had better make

arrangements to move your mother to a convalescent hospital within a day or so. She's taken a turn for the better, I think."

Move within a day? Where? How could I find a convalescent hospital in such a short time? More important, how does one select a convalescent hospital? All the horror stories I had ever heard about the treatment of the elderly in some of those facilities flooded my thoughts and I felt paralyzed with fear.

Would you know how to go about selecting a nursing home? I didn't know the first thing to do. Seeing my consternation and near panic, Dr. Cooper suggested I go to the head nurse for guidance. When I did she insisted that it was "against hospital policies to *recommend*" one hospital above another. She did, however, suggest several names.

Two of my brothers and I immediately began to check out all the facilities on the list. Most were far out of our reach financially. The nursing homes that we could afford left much to be desired. The staff appeared to be indifferent to our needs. The halls were so crowded with patients in wheelchairs we could hardly get through. Perhaps we could have overlooked the crowded conditions, but a strong stench immediately labeled the facilities unsatisfactory. Filled with anger and frustration I thought, *We're not looking for shelter for a pet! We need a place of comfort and security for our little mother!* I just didn't know what to do.

The fear of the unknown resulted in indescribable panic. My mother was obviously still ill and very weak. What were our options? How could we place Mom in a convalescent hospital and be assured she would be adequately cared for? Would the staff be kind? Would she be abused? Would they know what to do if her condition suddenly worsened? Would Mom understand why I could not take her home? Would she feel we had abandoned her? Fear completely erased all possibility that there were many good facilities available. All I could think about were the troubling questions: What to do? Where to turn? What should be our next step?

Mom had made her home with me for nine years prior to her surgery—a living arrangement that required great adjustments for both of us. But up to this point when Mom had a problem, either I or my brothers could "fix it." Now we were faced with a situation we could not fix. I couldn't take Mom back home after surgery because she still needed nursing care twenty-four hours a day. With the trauma and frustration came the big questions that played over and over in my heart and mind like a never-ending tape: *Why, Lord? Why does our godly mother have to go through this extended period of suffering?*

Looking back over that traumatic time in my life I still do not know why my mother had to go through all the pain, suffering and frustration while she was confined to a convalescent hospital for eight long years. I do know, however, that despite the heartaches I learned many valuable lessons during that time. Out of that experience comes the material for this book.

This is not the story of my mother, although I will refer to our experience from time to time. Rather, this is a book directed to the adult child who must care for an elderly parent or loved one. New discoveries and advancements in science, medicine and nutrition have extended people's life-spans to new limits. As a result, the need for caring for the elderly is becoming a reality as well as a heavy responsibility for many adult children. In some cases, these adult children are often people who themselves have advanced in years and are in need of *receiving* rather than *giving* care. In other situations, they are people who have growing children and family responsibilities of their own. My purpose is to help you, the adult child, find the guidance needed to make your role as a caregiver a little less traumatic. By sharing some of the answers I found to the questions that once overwhelmed me, perhaps I can help you avoid some of the pitfalls.

If you glanced briefly at the Contents page—or if you skipped over it entirely—go back again and look at the chapter headings carefully. Each chapter topic and issue was chosen with care so that you might find answers to some of the pressing problems you face, or will face, in the near future. Even if your parents are no longer living, this book will help you understand your own children better when advancing age forces you into the position where they become *your* caregivers.

Perhaps you have picked up this book because you are—or soon will be—involved in caring for your aged parents. Possibly you have already read other books authored by experts and specialists in the field of geriatrics. Why, then, should you read *this* book? Because it is written by a layperson who has already walked in the footsteps of a caregiver.

As you read this book imagine that you and I are sitting together and chatting. Let's talk about the problems you as the adult child face as you care for your elderly parent. Yes, there will be rough days ahead, but I believe you will find encouragement and help from the information written on the following pages. Be assured your situation of caregiving is not the end—there is hope because God will see you through.

How do I know? Because no matter what dips, chills and thrills came to me while I was on that emotional roller coaster, He was faithful to me by providing strength and guidance for each day.

Notes

1. All names and places mentioned in this book have been changed to protect the privacy of individuals involved.
2. Deuteronomy 33:25, *KJV*.

Chapter One
Caregiving Is Not for Cowards

If you have reached the age when the laugh lines in your face are no longer so funny and the once-distinguished gray at your temples is in need of Grecian Formula, you will be quick to admit that aging, like taxes, is a fact of life. Whether we like it or not, time passes all too quickly and it is no respecter of persons.

One day you suddenly realize that it is later than you think. You and your spouse have been busy climbing the ladder to success in your careers, buying a home and making house payments. As you are writing out another deposit slip for that college fund you have been working on for your children, it hits you. Your children—who were not yet in kindergarten when that fund started (wasn't that just a few weeks ago?)—are almost ready for high school!

Even as you are trying to figure out where the time has gone, you come face-to-face with yet another startling truth. Time has not stopped for your parents, either. They have aged. More and more, your parents seem to look to you for assistance in things they used to handle on their own. Now they are beginning to turn to you for advice—then usually fail to follow it. Without warning, you find yourself confronted with a new role of caring for aging parents who, because of advancing years, are no longer able to manage on their own.

Welcome to a growing group in our society that is encountering the same situation you are with your aging parents. You are, or soon will be, assuming the role of a caregiver for your elderly loved ones. Thanks to advancements in the fields of nutrition, science and medicine, our life expectancy has reached a new high. It is reported that by 1990 there will be an estimated 50,000 centenarians. According to the Metropolitan Life Insurance Company, that number will leap to 100,000 by the year 2000; by 2050 that figure could reach a total of 1 million 100-year-old men and women![1]

According to the United States Census Bureau, since the early 1960s the sixty-five-year-old and older population has grown twice as fast as the rest of our population. Statistics show there are almost 7 million Americans over the age of eighty today, and that number is expected to more than double by the year 2050.

In view of these studies the Census Bureau expressed real concern that "rapidly expanding numbers of older people represent a social phenomenon without historical precedent...[that] has various economic implications for individuals, families, policy-makers."

Without a doubt there will be few adult children whose lives will not be touched directly or indirectly by an aging loved one who needs some measure of care. For some that time will arise sooner than for others.

Aging Is Unpredictable

All people age at the same rate—one day at a time. Unlike child development, however, the aging process for adults does not follow a uniform pattern in each individual.

Remember when your children were babies? You learned to know about how old they would be when you could expect them to roll over and to sit up. You knew approximately at what age they would begin teething, crawling, walking, and thrilling you with their first words. Then with mixed emotions you sent them off to kindergarten at age four or five. The average growth patterns and developmental tasks are predictable in infants, children and teens.

Not so with the aging process. Aging, like the future, has no predictable pattern. Furthermore, it is sometimes difficult to identify the line that separates growing *up* from growing *old*. Of course, there are signs along the pathway of life that indicate aging is taking place. For example, when the newspaper print blurs a bit and people mumble far more than they used to, you can be rather positive both problems are an indication that the aging process has begun to take its toll.

If, however, you were to say to some sixty-year old, "Only five more years, my friend, and you're over the hill," that could be dangerous to your health—especially if you said it to someone like Charlie.

Charlie, a long-time friend of my family, was eighty at his last birthday, but he looks like a man in his sixties. He is retired, but Charlie has been a hard worker all his life. He is most contented when he is busy. Despite his age, Charlie does yard work for many elderly people, some who are younger than he.

The beautiful lawns and flowers in his neighborhood are proof of Charlie's pride in a job well done. Because he does such good, neat work, he has more requests for his services than he can handle.

Charlie is an avid reader, well-informed and conversant in many subjects. A warm, outgoing person, he is everyone's friend and a joy to have around.

God never meant for old age to be viewed as a curse. The Bible does not present old age as a condemnation, but neither does it idealize it.

In stark contrast to Charlie is Gus, who has talked of retirement for years. Gus is sixty-five but looks like a man in his eighties. He has no hobbies or interests; therefore, he has trouble whiling away all the leisure time he now has at retirement. He spends his days snacking and watching endless television programs. Gus refuses to follow the diet and exercise program prescribed by his physician. Angrily, Gus insists, "I've earned the right to relax and enjoy life." Although Gus claims he is enjoying life, his demeanor belies his claim.

His conversation, unlike Charlie's, is limited to complaints about the weather and to the aches and pains he says he experiences daily. For all practical purposes Gus has drawn the blinds on life. At age sixty-five, rather than enjoying life, he is a crotchety old man.

Age an Ogre?

Many younger people tend to have a negative concept of the aging process. They assume that life must be dreadful for the old. No doubt that negative concept is in part due to our society's emphasis on the health-kick fad of eating right to keep fit and trim. On the other hand, many elderly take old age surprisingly well.

Regardless of our attitude toward aging, most people confess to some fear. If a survey were conducted among adults, we would no doubt discover that one of the great fears of the elderly is that of becoming a burden to their children. The fear of the adult children would doubtless indicate a concern of how to care for their aged parents with the least amount of suffering. Do the passing years, then, condemn all of us to a life sentence of doom and fear of what lies ahead with the onslaught of age?

Contrary to popular belief concerning this stage of our lives, God never meant for old age to be viewed as a curse. The Bible does not present old age as a condemnation, but neither does it idealize it. On the contrary, the biblical description of advanced age in Ecclesiastes 12:1-5 is most vivid, and not too appealing.

Old age, according to the Scriptures, was a gift from God—a blessing, no less! "You shall live a long, good life; like standing grain, you'll not be harvested until it's time."[2] The Bible also presents age as a stage of honor: "Rise in the presence of the aged, show respect for the elderly and revere your God."[3] And with all due respect to our numerous brands of hair tints to hide our graying evidence, I remind you of the biblical view of gray hair: "Gray hair is a crown of splendor; it is attained [not by fear and worry, but] by a righteous life."[4]

The biblical view of age as demonstrated by many of the old patriarchs was that age was part of life. In his book *As Our Years Increase,* author Tim Stafford refers to the psalmist's view of old age, saying that, "Old age is good, good even if hard. It is good because it is part of life because God made it...because God is in it."[5]

Before he died, my father experienced tremendous suffering as a result of cancer. When he was first diagnosed as having cancer, one of the verses Dad frequently quoted was, "I will not die but live, and will proclaim what the Lord has done."[6] And he did. As the years of suffering slipped by, my father was able to accept the inevitable. A few weeks before his death his pastor called on Dad at my parents' home. During his visit the minister expressed sympathy and concern for Dad's suffering. Looking back at my father's response I believe Dad understood the biblical view of age—and of life. Dad's response to the minister's concern was, "Pastor, when I see Jesus face-to-face it will be worth it all."

Age and its frequent by-product of caregiving does not mean you have been sentenced to hard labor. Yes, caregiving *is* hard work—anyone involved in the task will vouch for that truth! However, caregiving does not have to be depressing or unrewarding or devoid of joy. Despite their age, your parents do not lose their individual personalities. They are still people with feelings, opinions and ideas. They still need love, respect, compassion, understanding and friendship—needs common to any human being. Keep these qualities and needs in mind, and caregiving can also be rewarding.

Prepare for Caregiving

To become aware that an aging loved one will soon need additional care can be challenging to some families, while disconcerting and frightening to others. Most families want to help, but the question often is how to do so effectively when there are so many problems that appear with old age.

The differences in the aging process, as we have noted in the examples of Charlie and Gus and the way the two men responded to aging, represent something of the problems adult children face in caring for parents and loved ones who are slowly becoming disabled. If all elderly people were like Charlie, our task would be easier. But they are not. We are dealing with individuals, not with a programmed or mechanical group who responds on cue. Each aging adult is a person of worth. Each has his or her own unique physical condition, habits, background and emotional temperament.

An important factor in facing caregiving is to prepare and plan ahead as much as possible. The most common response I hear from an adult child when the subject of caring for an aging loved one comes into a conversation is, "Yes, I know. My mother (father) is getting up there in years, too. But I don't even want to think about it, or about what we'll do when she (he) can no longer live alone."

Most of us, however, tend to spend time and energy planning for everything else in our lives. We plan for our careers, for the children's education, for vacations, for investments and security. Some of us even make extensive plans for a comfortable, worry-free retirement. Yet, despite our well-planned lives and long-range goals, many of us are caught by surprise when our aging parents suddenly suffer from a serious illness and are in need of extended care. And when faced with that traumatic physical problem, we tend to panic—as I did when we were faced with the need to move my mother from an acute care hospital to a convalescent home.

Examine Your Own Feelings

Part of preparation and planning involves your own feelings. Of course, you need to understand your aging parents' needs before you can adequately care for them. Of equal importance, however, is that you understand yourself and your own feelings. How do you feel when you recognize the first indication that old age is sneaking up on *you*? Do you ignore it? Deny it? Or can you face the fact that old age, like birth, is a fact of life?

Do you believe that old age means your productivity and creativity comes to a screeching halt? Or that after sixty-five-plus there is nothing worthwhile in life for you? If so, you are dead wrong! To believe that old age means an end to all enjoyment and usefulness can only result in self-pity, depression, ill health and grief. At the age of fifty-two, the English poet Robert Browning wrote these famous lines:

> Grow old along with me! The best is yet to be
> The last of life, for which the first was made;
> Our times are in His hands.[7]

Examine your own feelings carefully. Is old age the end? Or is it your belief that our times *are* in God's hands? If you agree with Browning, as I do, you will be able to deal more adequately with the difficulties and heartaches of old age, whether your own or that of an aging loved one. How can I be so sure? Because of a promise from One who always keeps His word. He said, "Listen to me...you whom I have *upheld* since you were conceived, and have carried since your birth. Even to your old age and gray hairs I am he, I am he who will *sustain* you. I have made you and I will *carry* you; I will sustain you and I will *rescue* you."[8] There is help available for you from Him.

In doing research before writing this book I tried to evaluate common feelings we have about our elderly parents. I asked a number of adult children three questions: (1) What were your feelings when you first noticed through some act, response or gesture that your parents were getting old? (2) How do you feel when you consider that your role may change from being your parents' child to your parents' caregiver? (3) What has been your relation with your parents? Have you been friends, or has there been estrangement? Let's look at each question, as well as some of the answers I received.

My Parents Old? Never!

Question one: What were your feelings when you first noticed your parents were getting old? I found that most adult children experience feelings of sadness, regret, anger, fear, threat, shock and denial. Without hesitation one daughter said, "I wanted to stop time so they wouldn't get older."

The child, whom psychologists tell us lies buried

deep within the hearts of each adult, has always thought of parents as being indestructible and available at all times to meet our needs and solve our problems. Now, however, we realize that old age is about to rob us of the prop that we have depended upon, and the result is the variety of emotional feelings mentioned above.

How well I remember the time the doctor suggested it would be wise for my father to stop driving his own car. Of course, I realized the doctor was correct. I knew it was better, not only for my father's safety but also for the well-being of all other persons who shared the streets and freeways with this elderly man. Nevertheless, I cried. I felt anger, a deep hurt and sadness at this definite evidence of Dad's aging. I knew that losing his driving privileges meant losing a portion of his independence. That loss was a big blow to Dad. In time, however, he seemed to adjust, at least outwardly—better, in fact, than I did.

Me in Charge? No Way!

Question two: How do you feel when you consider that your role may change from being your parents' child to their caregiver? This was perhaps the stickiest of the three questions. One reason it is difficult is that in Christian homes children are taught at an early age to love, honor and respect their parents. With the changing role we tend to become confused about honor and respect.

Perhaps that was one of the main reasons I had problems as I realized my mother was becoming more and more dependent upon me. My feelings slid up and down an emotional scale, registering pity, resentment, anger, frustration and sadness—all mixed up with love. I did not want the role of "taking charge." I did not like it. Selfishly, I wanted my mother to continue in her familiar, independent, optimistic role as the strong encourager of my childhood. Nor did I want to lose the unique friendship we had developed as adults.

I felt guilty because everyone knows a Christian daughter should not have the feelings toward a parent that I was experiencing. Chiding myself only increased my guilt and failed to erase my negative feel-

Honoring a parent means we are to esteem them for who they are and for what they have done....*We honor them by assisting them when needed.*

ings. Not until I heard a lecture by a professional in the field of geriatrics did I understand that my feelings were very common for people in my situation. The realization did not completely solve my problem, but I realize now, with hindsight, it was a beginning—an important beginning—in accepting a necessary change in my attitude and thinking.

Recognizing a truth and acting upon that truth, however, usually takes time as we try to work through a confusing problem and its ramifications. Therefore, when the adult child finds him- or herself in a situation where roles are being reversed from being dependent to caring for a parent, the confusing questions related to honoring our parents are not often solved immediately.

Dr. Judith Alexandre, family counselor of the B.F.C. Counseling Center in Ventura, California, discussed with me the confusion of honoring and respecting a parent in an adult child's changing role. Dr. Alexandre agrees with me that the Bible teaches that children are not to neglect their aged parents. We are to honor them. She stressed, however, the importance of defining what is meant by honoring our parents.

I found that both the Hebrew and Greek meaning for the word "honor" as used in Exodus 20:12 and Ephesians 6:2 is to obey, to respect, to value, to esteem due to virtue, wisdom and reputation.[9]

As we talked about how the adult child honors his or her parent, Dr. Alexandre's concept was especially helpful in view of the original meaning of the word. She said, in effect, that honoring a parent means *we are to esteem them for who they are and for what they have done*. It does not mean, however, that the adult child's life or the life and care of a spouse or children must be sacrificed at the expense of caring for an aged parent.

Author Tim Stafford also referred to the need to define the word "honor," and he points out that the root word in Hebrew is "weight." In light of that definition, Stafford says we honor our parents by the lives that we live, lives that reflect discipline and wisdom that would make a parent proud, thereby giving our parents weight in our community. We honor them by assisting them when needed. Finally, we honor the memory of our parents, even though the last days of aging may have been difficult, by recalling the good times in our past.[10]

Friend or Foe?

Question three: Have you and your parents been friends, or has there been estrangement in your relationship? Most adult children answered this question by saying that, for the most part, there had been a warm and friendly attitude. Others, however, admitted there had been some friction. These persons now find themselves confronted with another problem in caregiving—that of caring for someone they really don't like too well.

Pat, who is in her late forties, said, "My mother and I have never been friends." She went on to admit she always felt that she was a disappointment to her mother. "It seemed," Pat said, "I could never quite come up to her expectations. I wanted her approval so badly, but..." As she talked, Pat brushed tears from her eyes and I knew without being told that she loved her mother deeply, but still suffered from parental rejection. Even as a middle-aged daughter, Pat was still missing that approval she had worked for all her life. According to Pat's close friends, her aged mother is known as a very dominating, self-centered person.

To harbor hostile or hurt feelings can only lead to more heartaches. There comes a time when feelings of estrangement toward parents must be dealt with. Failure to deal with the rift or squelching hostile feelings instead of discussing them with your parents will lead to deep resentment. That resentment often grows while you are under the pressure of caring for your loved one in addition to maintaining your own family responsibilities. The problems may not vanish overnight by airing them, but they must be resolved. Earnestly pray about your own attitude. Ask the Lord to help you as you honestly examine your own heart for wrongs that you should right. Then pray for a God-appointed opportunity for a frank but loving talk with your parents.

Above all else, when feelings of guilt threaten to overwhelm and crush you because of an unfortunate broken relationship, try to commit these guilty feelings to Him also. It may be necessary to talk to a counselor who will be able to help you sort through your feelings, so that your hurts may heal and you may have a more realistic and healthy feeling about yourself as well as about your parents.

Before you attempt to place blame for a poor relationship between you and your parents, remember that behavior is a complex process. In some cases frustration, illness, fear or frailties may cause once charming personalities to become warped or to disappear altogether. As a result, the elderly then tend to become a little less likable.

As people advance in age the personality traits that were a bit annoying in the past often become more pronounced and, therefore, create friction and frustration, placing even more stress and strain on the adult children. Let me assure you, however, there is hope and life *after* caregiving. Go on trusting in the One who has promised to supply all your needs "according to his glorious riches in Christ Jesus."[11]

Notes

1. Bard Lindeman, "It's True: Americans Are Getting Older," *Ventura County Star-Free Press Vista* magazine, October 2, 1988, p.8.
2. Job 5:26, *TLB*.

3. Leviticus 19:32.
4. Proverbs 16:31.
5. Tim Stafford, *As Our Years Increase* (Grand Rapids, MI: Pyranee Books published by Zondervan Publishing House, 1989), p.31.
6. Psalm 118:17.
7. Robert Browning, "Rabbi Ben Ezra," 1864, Public domain.
8. Isaiah 46:3,4, italics added.
9. *Matthew Henry's Commentary* (Old Tappen, NJ: Fleming H. Revell), vol. 1 (revised); and Merrill F. Unger, *Unger's Bible Dictionary* (Moody Press, Chicago, 1957).
10. Tim Stafford, *As Our Years Increase* (Grand Rapids, MI: Pyranee Books published by Zondervan Publishing House, 1989), p. 243.
11. Philippians 4:19.

Chapter Two

Fears and Losses of the Elderly

Television comedian Flip Wilson once said that if we had our entire lives to live over again we probably would not have the strength. As we chuckle and nod in agreement, we are quick to admit that we often feel worn out by our exhausting life-styles and the changes—some more traumatic than others—that life tosses our way.

The American author Carl Sandburg expressed his feelings about life by saying:

> Life is like an onion.
> You peel it off
> One layer at a time
> And sometimes you cry a little.[1]

Sandburg's homespun analogy is a picture of the changes and losses being peeled off "one layer at a time" by the advancing years.

Fears and Losses of the Elderly

Psychologists tell us that all of life is made up of continuous changes from childhood all the way to old age. Surprising as it may seem, the last twenty years of life—that stage we call old age—bring almost as many changes as do the first twenty. Changes in the latter part of life are usually more frightening than changes in the first twenty years because they carry the threat of loss, disability or other degeneration.

In the previous chapter we looked at how adult children feel about their elderly parents. In this chapter we want to consider what is really happening to the elderly. How do our parents feel about what is happening to them?

A very wise king once said that, as a man thinks within himself, so is he.[2] The good news is that a glimmer of a new attitude has surfaced that says getting older is getting better. Results of this new attitude seem to cause all of us to take a second look at some of the misconceptions and prejudices of what life is like for people in their later sixties and seventies.

Because of better health in later years, many of the elderly are happy. They accept their limitations and, despite advancing years, they become excellent role models for being happy, productive individuals.

Interesting surveys have been done recently on how the elderly think of themselves. One study by two researchers, Tuckmann and Lorge, done on a group of persons who were *more* than eighty years old, indicated the following. Of the group surveyed, 36 percent considered themselves to be middle-aged, 11 percent felt they were young, while 53 percent admitted they felt they were old.[3]

Bard Lindeman, whose column, "In Your Prime," appears each week in the Sunday issue of the *Ventura*

County Star-Free Press Vista magazine, conducted a survey of 411 women ranging in age from thirty to sixty-nine. In that study only 3 percent of the women said they felt that they were elderly, while 50.2 percent—more than half—considered themselves to be young! Four percent were a bit more conservative by classifying themselves as being middle-aged.[4]

Despite this new attitude, however, there is no denying the fact that advancing years do eventually bring some degree of loss as they affect physical abilities and health. When the elderly become aware of these losses, either in themselves or among their friends, fears do begin to surface and nag.

What's It Like to Be Old?

What word pictures flash into your mind when you hear the terms "elderly" or "old age"? Depending upon our own age, most of us tend to associate the elderly with such terms as poor, unoccupied, sick, lonely, unproductive and dejected.

In an attempt to discover what it is like to be old, a young lady named Pat Moore launched a fascinating, thorough research in 1979 to supplement her studies in gerontology and industrial designs. With the help of a professional make-up artist, twenty-six-year-old Pat Moore disguised herself as an eighty-year-old woman with a gray wig and latex wrinkles. To get a more realistic concept of living in a body that had stiffened joints, she wore bandages and splints under her clothing. Moore disguised herself to represent three different life-styles: (1) a lady on a fixed income, (2) a bag lady, and (3) a woman of wealth. For three years she donned her disguises and mingled with the public as she traveled across our land.

Pat Moore describes her adventure into the senior world in her book entitled *Disguised*.[5] While there were positive experiences when she was treated with concern and respect, there were many more times when she was lonely and very frightened. She was repeatedly ignored; she was shoved, mugged and even short-changed while disguised as a lady on a fixed income. Moore discovered that how a senior citizen is treated in our society depends, unfortunately, on the amount of money one has.

To me, the most discouraging and startling account was her report of attending a conference on gerontology conducted by some of her *own* co-workers. So good was her disguise that she was not recognized. The very people who were meeting to discover new and better methods of working with the elderly treated Moore with a great deal of disrespect, even ignoring her at times.

In summing up the result of her adventure, Pat Moore urges her readers to look past the wrinkles and the stereotypes so frequently associated with the elderly, and to look instead at the individual. She maintains that we are responsible for one another. "People must know they don't have to fear their own aging, or that of the people they love," says Pat who, after her adventure, founded Moore and Associates, a company that specializes in age-related projects.

Her message to senior citizens who are treated in a shabby manner is for them to protest. Pat encourages those who are slow to accept her challenge, to protest for their own sake, because in doing so they are doing it for others, as well.[6]

We can't all put on a disguise as Pat Moore did, but we need to recognize that old age is a fact of life. While many older people are able to manage well on their own, by looking at some of the fears, concerns and losses prevalent to many elderly, you as the adult child are better able to understand when, or if, some of these fears become a problem in your family.

The young at heart...will experience a satisfying, contented old age despite their handicaps, while self-centered, unhappy persons will be despondent and perhaps totally dependent.

Fears that Come with Aging

We need to recognize that fears vary at different stages of life. When six-year-old Bobby displayed obvious misgivings and anxiety about starting first grade, his mother questioned him with little success. She pointed out the fun, the exciting new activities and new adventures in store.

Finally, Bobby verbalized his concern. "I don't want to go to school," he said, "'cause I don't want my teeth to fall out like Timmy's did when he started school."

Just as Bobby's fear was unique to him at age six, so adult children and the elderly also have fears unique to their particular situations. Some fears, within reason, are normal. If a person has just gone through surgery for cancer or has been told he is losing his hearing or eyesight, he has a right to be fearful and to wonder how he will manage. Other fears, however, are a little like Bobby's. For a six-year-old to lose his baby teeth is part of growing up, just as the losses that come with aging are part of the natural life-cycle. All adults need to adapt to the normal physical decline that comes with advancing years. However, nothing in the world ages us as much as a troubled mind. Therefore, we need to identify fears that are normal and to recognize that many fears common to people fifty years old and older are, in fact, myths.

The Fear of Frailty

One big myth of aging, according to gerontology experts, is the frailty of the elderly. Dr. B. Oliver, while speaking at the 1981 Conference on Aging, reminded his listeners that only 5 percent of the elderly are living in nursing homes or other extended care facilities at any one time.[7]

No one will deny that our parents are more vulnerable to the threats of disability and death from long-term illnesses, but younger people are not exempt from these threats either. In their book, authors Barbara Silverstone and Helen K. Hyman report that the elderly average less than fifteen days a year in bed due to illness.[8] Scientific surveys show that, even after sixty-five, many illnesses and disabilities common to the elderly can be cured or arrested before the ailments become chronic. Despite these statistics there are, of course, still many older people who live with a variety of chronic but treatable diseases. The encouraging note is that only about 15 percent of these persons are physically incapable of continuing their normal activities.[9]

Currently, 28 million people over the age of sixty-five live in the United States. Dr. Alvin F. Poussaint indicates that, contrary to the false belief that most of these elderly people are confined in extended care facilities, 95 percent live in the community and most of them manage their own households.[10]

In view of these statistics, adult children as well as the elderly need to recognize that old age itself is not the problem. If we agree with the wisdom of King Solomon that as a man thinks in his heart so is he, the bottom line is how well you and your parents are able to adapt to the losses that life brings. The young at heart—regardless of physical age—will experience a satisfying, contented old age despite their handicaps, while self- centered, unhappy persons will be despondent and perhaps even totally dependent. Studies show that most elderly persons adjust rather well to the changes that come with old age. Most seem to realize that aging is the final act in the stage of living.

Fear of Change

Not only the elderly but most adults dislike change. At the risk of becoming rigid, we tend to find a familiar routine and settle down with it, even though that routine may in time become nothing more than a comfortable but nonproductive rut.

The middle-aged employee frequently experiences a mixture of emotions when new technology is introduced at his work place. He feels challenged, but often there is also fear. What if he is replaced by machines? What if he can't hack it and keep up with the younger, more vibrant workers? But change is a truism. No matter how threatening today's world of high technology and computers, we must admit that to stay in the working world we must roll with the punches and accept change.

Realizing how threatening change can be to us, we need to try to identify with the elderly and the changes they face. By identifying with them it will be somewhat easier to understand their fears. They too fear changes. They fear the time when they may no longer be needed by their families. Unfortunately, many of the fears confronting the elderly often boil down to very real losses. Let's examine some of these losses.

Loss of Identity

One of the first losses for the older person comes at retirement. We tend to identify ourselves by our professions. We are teachers, nurses, mechanics or bookkeepers. At retirement the loss of that professional identity begins to nibble at the retiree. Questions that haunt many retired people are: Who am I now? How do I identify myself? For some that loss becomes so serious that it erodes or even destroys their self-image.

In addition to the loss of professional identity, older people often are the recipients of a prejudice that psychologists and psychiatrists call "ageism." It is a prejudice that is as mean, senseless, destructive and disabling as any other form of intolerance. An excellent definition of ageism was given by one senior citizen who said that she was treated as though she were invisible.

Dr. Robert Coles, psychiatrist and author at Harvard University, told of a woman who fought and overcame ageism. A young salesperson had ignored the woman at a department store and did not wait on her. When the lady complained to her son, he wasn't much help and felt there was little she could do.

The woman was old, but apparently she was a fighter. She was not about to give up on herself. In effect she said, "If I think of myself as nothing, then I am *through!*" She realized that it all comes down to how you feel about yourself and about life.

One day she returned to the same department store only to have the pattern of being ignored repeated. This time, with a smile and a great deal of spunk, she said, "All right, sir. Now that you've had your kicks with the young, how about waiting on one of us who is not so young?"

Dr. Cole reported that her response worked. The salesperson was a bit surprised but, seeing the twinkle in her eye, he gave her his full attention. Because she saw herself with some respect and had a good self-image, explained Dr. Cole, she suddenly became visible.[11]

The good news is that all believers in Christ—the caregivers as well as the elderly—are always visible to the heavenly Father. Do you realize that you will never lose your identity with Him, whether you are sixteen, sixty or ninety-six? You are now and always will be a child of God and a member of His family.[12] Furthermore, you are an heir—heir of God and co-heir with Christ.[13] I can't think of a better identity, can you?

Loss of Mobility

Mobility is something most of us take for granted —we do, that is, until we lose it. Think for a moment how you feel when your car needs to be in the garage for a day or two for repairs. Frustrating, isn't it? Especially in places like Southern California where commuter buses are very scarce! Without a car you are grounded.

That must be the way the elderly driver feels when he realizes that the day will soon come when he can no longer operate his own automobile. To accept that knowledge is even more painful because, at that age, the loss is permanent.

Recently the popular documentary television program "20/20" considered the problem of the older driver. They discussed the question: When is a person too old to drive?

Researchers for the program indicated that after age seventy-five the accident rate increased. The reason? Driving involves three important areas that deteriorate with age: eyesight, hearing and the ability to make quick decisions. As a result of this physical deterioration, older people have trouble judging the speed and distance of oncoming traffic. They hesitate a moment too long and many have accidents involving left turns.

To lose the mobility of driving hurts. One older man interviewed on "20/20" indicated that, to him, giving up driving was like losing his right arm. Others said they would rather die than stop driving.

The answer to the question posed on the program was that it is not the *age* of the individual but the *level of impairment* that is the bottom line for giving up driving.

What can be done to help the elderly maintain safe driving habits? The concensus of the researchers on the television program was that training courses to brush up on road and driving laws are helpful. Also, getting the family involved can be a positive step because, through love and compassion, they may be

---

Most doctors agree that recovery for those who are ill is far more dependent on overall health than on the age of the patient.

---

able to encourage the oldster to give up his license on his own.

If you feel your parent should no longer be driving and the above suggestions have not been successful, you may want to talk to your parent's doctor. Some—though certainly not all—doctors will insist that the person stop driving because of health reasons.

Failure to get a license renewed and being unable to drive is often the first phase of the loss of mobility. A deteriorating body ravished by such diseases as arthritis or osteoporosis, where the bones of the elderly become brittle and susceptible to fracture, means an even greater loss of physical mobility.

Loss of Physical Health

Older people should be encouraged to take care of their health, but this does not mean that health care is to become an all consuming activity. All ages need to beware of excessive concern with imagined complaints, which can turn into imagined ills or neurotic behavior.

For example, her first pair of bifocals sent fifty-five-year-old Betty into a tailspin. As a registered nurse she was well aware that aging meant her eyes were becoming rigid and inflexible. If this deterioration was happening in her eyes, Betty worried, was it also happening to the rest of her body? The worry became an obsession. She talked for weeks about her bifocals and was positive that the next step after bifocals would be cataracts and, finally, a complete loss of vision.

Modern medicine and science have advanced to such an extent that many of the disabilities that come with aging are far less threatening now than ever before. People in their eighties and even nineties remain in fairly good health. The medical profession, on the whole, places emphasis on the elderly maintaining wellness. Most doctors agree that recovery for those who are ill is far more dependent on overall health than on the age of the patient. Many hospitals indicate that when selecting options for treatments they consider the general health of the patient, rather than age.

A good health plan for the elderly includes maintaining proper diets, exercise, rest, relaxation and regular medical check-ups. In addition to a physical fitness program, the elderly need to remain in contact

with the world around them through social relationships. Two registered nurses, Paula D. Thomas and
Elizabeth M. Hooper of the University of New Mexico
School of Medicine in Albuquerque, did some interesting research with a group of seventy-two-year-old
men and women. It was found that the healthiest
elders were those who had satisfying social lives,
including frequent contacts with friends and acquain-
tances. These people felt they were still in control of
their lives as a result of these contacts, and could take
better care of themselves. While Thomas and Hooper
indicated their research could not absolutely prove
that contact with others causes good health, there is a
strong feeling that social activities contribute to
healthier seniors.[14]

Could it be that this was what wise King Solomon
was talking about when he said, "A cheerful heart is
good medicine, but a crushed spirit dries up the
bones"?[15]

Loss of Mental Stability

Have you ever made out a grocery list or a "to-do" list
and then forgot where you put it? Who hasn't? Even
though loss of memory is often associated with the
aging process, forgetfulness does not mean it's time to
push the panic button. In fact, some people—perhaps
those who believe the adage "You can't teach an old
dog new tricks"—are convinced that learning stops
after a certain age. That concept is a myth. Educators
and medical experts have proven that learning never
stops. The learning process slows down with age but
the ability to learn goes on. Gerontologists encourage
the middle-aged and oldsters to stay mentally alert by

"exercising" their brains. Just as failing to use muscles of an arm or leg leads to stiffness and weakness, so failing to use the brain can lead to mental atrophy. In other words, the experts are telling us that we are really not *losing* it, we just may not be *using* it as often as we once did.

All of us, therefore, who have reached the age of fifty-plus need to pursue mental activities. If we are to stay mentally alert, we need to read, memorize Scripture, work crossword puzzles, and be involved in—or at least, aware of—the issues facing our society and those things going on in the world around us.

Many retired senior citizens go back to school and enroll in courses they have long been interested in but never had time for. Some of the courses are "mind stretchers," while others—like photography or cake decorating—are for fun.

The loss of mental stability is perhaps one of the most frightening ogres of growing old. Dementing diseases know no barriers, and people from all walks of life have suffered from them. If a dementing disease strikes your loved one, there is no reason to feel humiliated or embarrassed.

Older people often experience depression; as a result, there can be memory loss, confusion and other mental problems. Depression is often a cover-up for other problems such as deep grief, severe guilt, shame, unresolved anger or even something as simple as a lack of a proper diet. Fortunately, mental disturbances caused by this type of depression are not irreversible. The patient's memory improves greatly when the cause of depression and the depression itself is treated.

At one time it was generally accepted that senility affected all older people. Medical science, however, disagrees with that concept now. Studies show that only 5-8 percent of the elderly show severe intellectual impairment, and about the same percentage suffer from milder impairment. Of course, mental diseases become more prevalent in persons who live to be in their eighties and nineties; but even in that group, 80 percent never experience a significant memory loss or other mental problems.[16] No one would deny that some memory loss is common for the elderly, but it is usually not enough to interfere with their lives.

Loss of the Familiar

We dare not underestimate the importance of friends in the lives of the elderly. Their peers are the ones who clearly understand our loved ones and are quick to sympathize. When an elderly person sees friends and relatives become ill and die or move away to an extended care facility, there is a deep, haunting fear of isolation, plus the fear of what further changes may be just around the corner.

Ours is a mobile society. Transfers to new jobs mean adult children and friends move away. Neighborhoods change and become unsafe for the elderly. Advancing years and poor health frequently mean a move from a familiar home saturated with fond memories of younger years.

While most elderly realize that changes are inevitable, the loss of the familiar can, nevertheless, be traumatic for even the strongest oldster. Kind understanding, support and love are most important for the elderly at that time when the familiar begins to slip away.

Loss of Financial Security

Two subjects that are often very awkward and touchy to discuss, even among the closest families, are money and death. How about your family? Are your parents open to the idea of having you become acquainted with their financial status?

If both of your parents are living, encourage the one who handled the finances to acquaint the spouse with the family finances. Financial know-how is important for both spouses. If you are invited to hear the financial information, fine. But at least both parents should be aware of such family money matters as budgets, debts, mortgages, investments, insurance policies, IRAs and pensions. Both should know about the contents of a will. Many widows have been plunged into even greater trauma at the death of a spouse because of the overwhelming confusion and fear of the unknown financial how-to, added to the grief of the loss of her loved one. Financial consultants often advise healthy, alert senior citizens to assign a power of attorney now, to become effective if and when the elderly become infirm. (The power of attorney will be discussed more fully in chapter 8.)

Without destroying the dignity of your parents by insinuating that the time has come for you to take over their finances because they are no longer capable, discuss finances with them if they are open to it. If they are unwilling to discuss money matters, you cannot force them to do so. You can, however, inform yourself of the various financial aids available for the elderly in your state as well as nationwide, find out who is eligible to receive funds and how to apply for funds when the need arises. Being well informed before a crisis will prevent much heartache later. An important note to remember is that the entire financial situation for the elderly is in a state of flux. Laws change frequently. You need to be alert and stay informed.

Summary

Much of my adult life and formal training was devoted to working with children. An important truth I learned was that, in order to help each child to the best of my ability, I had to know the needs of that child—what made him or her tick. That truism, I believe, is also necessary for adult children and those who work with the elderly. If we know their needs and can identify some of their fears and concerns, we will become much more effective in our care, and the elderly will be much happier.

Notes

1. *Who Cares? Helpful Hints for Those Who Care for a Dependent Older Person at Home,* published by The Andrus Volunteers, University of Southern California, Los Angeles, 1985.
2. Proverbs 23:7, *KJV*
3. Tim Stafford, *As Our Years Increase* (Grand Rapids, MI: Pyranee Books published by Zondervan Pub. House, 1989), p.15.
4. Marie Lakin, "29something," *Ventura County Star-Free Press Vista* magazine, August 6, 1989.
5. Pat Moore with Charles Paul Conn, *Disguised* (Waco, TX: Word Books, 1985).
6. Ibid. p.173.
7. David B. Oliver, *Ministering to the Aged* (Pomona, CA: Focus on the Family, 1984).
8. Barbara Silverstone & Helen Kandel Hyman, *You and Your Aging Parent* (New York: Pantheon Books, 1982).
9. Ibid.
10. Alvin F. Poussaint, M.D., "Introduction," *Time Flies,* Bill Cosby (New York: Bantam Books, 1988).
11. Bard Lindeman, "In Your Prime," *Ventura County Star-Free Press Vista* magazine, January 8, 1989, p.14.

12. John 1:12, Romans 8:16.
13. Romans 8:17.
14. Michael Briley, "Positive Thinking: A Way to Stay Healthy," *Modern Maturity* magazine, (Publication of the American Association of Retired Persons), vol. 27, No. 4, August-September 1984.
15. Proverbs 17:22.
16. Nancy L. Mace and Peter V. Robins, M.D., *The 36-Hour Day* (Baltimore: The Johns Hopkins University Press, 1981).

Chapter Three
Too Soon to Quit!

"If I have my health and a clear mind, it won't bother me to get old."

"When I reach seventy, I hope I can be as vibrant as she is!"

"My parents are driving me crazy now that Dad's retired! They have nothing to do, so they bug us! Why don't they go out with their own friends?"

"Mom makes me feel so guilty when she acts hurt because we don't include her in *everything* we do!"

The consensus of adult children is reflected in some of the comments they made as we talked about their parents and getting old. Recall the two men, Charlie and Gus, whom I mentioned in chapter 1. Both had a different concept of the meaning of aging and retirement. Sixty-five-year-old Gus has withdrawn from life. Although he wants to relax and enjoy his leisure, he is bored and miserable. Vibrant, vivacious eighty-year-old Charlie, on the other hand, is busy, happy and apparently pulsating with life. His children are concerned that he might be too busy for his own good, but Charlie insists, "It's too soon to quit!"

The psalmist drops a hint about the aged and paints a word picture of the elderly person who has walked with God: "They will *still bear fruit in old age, they will stay fresh and green.*"[1] A similar idea comes from the great American historian Thomas Cole who viewed old age, not only as a time of completing a long journey and preparing for death, but also a time of service to family and community as a result of a long, fruitful life.

Think of the advancements that have occurred during our parents' life-span in the fields of medicine, communication and travel. Now think of the accumulated wisdom Christian parents have gathered from their sixty-five-plus years of walking with the Lord. A former editor is quoted in *Christianity Today* as saying, "Retirement is not the end of being, but the continuation of becoming the perfect reflection of Jesus Christ."[2]

Some of the most interesting and challenging older people I have known are those over sixty-five who resent being lumped with others in a chronological sameness. And, of course, they have the right idea. Due to the diverse attitudes, abilities and physical condition among the over sixty-five group, it is impossible to accurately designate them into one age level. Many, like Charlie, agree it's too soon to quit.

Eunice, for example, is in her mid-seventies, a widow who has been battling cancer for a number of years. But she doesn't waste time feeling sorry for herself—she's too busy! She says she helps the "older" people in her neighborhood, she travels, volunteers her services to such senior citizens' agencies as Meals-on-Wheels and is involved in her church. Her children and grandchildren have all moved to other states, but that does not keep Eunice from enjoying her offspring. Despite numerous hospital confinements, she is always able to convince her doctors that she is able to travel to visit her family.

Eunice is frugal and takes advantage of reduced air fares. When her friends at the travel agency quoted a price before her last visit to see her children in California, she challenged them. With a chuckle in her "take-charge" voice she said, "You've got to find a better price than that! Call me when you do." And they did!

Her daughter told me that after Eunice returned to her home back east, her doctors admitted she was right. Despite their apprehension, the trip had indeed been good for her.

Involvement for Parents? Why?

Perhaps you are thinking: My parents have worked hard all their lives. Let them lean back and take life easy—they've earned it! Why insist on keeping them involved?

You're right—our parents should be allowed to slow down and enjoy life. Involvement does not mean they continue at the same pace as pre-retirement days. If, however, an older person has no reason to get up each morning, he will sleep late and lounge aimlessly all day. His exercise will dwindle to moving from the TV to the dinner table and back to his favorite Wall-hugger, where he will nap most of the afternoon or evening. He will become lethargic and dull. That person will be so wrapped up in himself he will become a bore with nothing to talk about but his own gripes and pains. Before he speaks, you know what the conversation will be—it's always the same. There is nothing to stimulate his thinking or interests. Inactivity, both physical and mental, spells T-R-O-U-B-L-E. Therefore, we need to encourage involvement with life because that can extend the elderly's independence for many years. No motivation is needed for persons as active as Eunice. All that is necessary is to stay in touch, encourage and enjoy them. I am not an avid fan of bumper stickers, but I appreciate the one seen on vans or campers driven by elderly couples that proclaims, "We are spending our children's inheritance." My response is, "Go for it—with all the gusto you can muster!"

Overcoming Withdrawal

A concern that is frequently expressed by caring adult children is *how* to get their parents involved. Despite the efforts children make, some parents refuse to cooperate. Yet there are telltale clues that these parents are beginning to vegetate and to withdraw into their own little worlds. Why is it so difficult to get them involved?

Numerous reasons could be listed. Many elderly find it difficult to discover and develop major new interests. Despite his adventuresome spirit as a young man, Winston Churchill once said, "It is hard to find new interests at the end of one's life."

Some parents may be a bit shy about new ventures because of the fear of the unknown. Others may lack the drive they once had and are, therefore, harder to motivate as they insist they "don't want the hassle." When I questioned family counselor Dr. Judith Alexandre about the involvement problem, she reminded me that we must not lose sight of the dignity of each individual. As individuals our parents have every right to say no to our suggestions. We have no right to force them to follow our ideas, no matter how well-meaning or how loving our concern. Alexandre's advice was to present the options and permit the elderly to choose to accept or decline.

An important first step to help parents become

Opportunities for involvement are numerous and almost unlimited. People who look for a way to become involved usually find it.

---

involved and to maintain an active life-style is to know their interests. To encourage your parents to go whale-watching with the seniors from your church would be ludicrous if they hate the ocean and become seasick at the sight of water. If, however, they are interested in gardening, you no doubt will have more success by suggesting a visit to a flower or garden show.

Find out what is available in your community. If an activity sounds promising, talk to others who have participated or check it out by going to the activity yourself. Don't push too hard. Give your parents time to talk over your suggestions. Listen to them and try to discover why they are hesitant. They will respond better given time to make their own decisions without feeling you are coercing them into an activity they both dislike. The key is to find that balance of providing suggestions and available options, while allowing them the freedom to accept or to decline. A hassle? Perhaps, but remember, gerontologists say that any time and effort put into helping the aged to remain active has the rich reward of keeping them independent and healthy as long as possible.

Opportunities Galore

Opportunities for involvement are numerous and almost unlimited. People who look for a way to become involved usually find it. And people who —despite arthritis, failing eyesight and other ravages of old age—still display a genuine interest in others seldom complain or wallow in self-pity. They always appear to be happiest when they find a way to help someone who needs help more than they do themselves.

Volunteer Work

Many retired persons have found volunteer work most rewarding. To the person who needs to feel needed (and who doesn't?), volunteer work is the answer. In the past years a great gap in volunteer ranks has developed because so many women have joined the work force. Who better to fill that void than able-bodied retired men and women?

Numerous volunteers have found new challenges in a variety of different fields, as well as great satisfaction in filling a void. Some have found that volunteering is a way to continue a professional talent, while others have found a challenging *new* career. One happy sixty-five-year-old expressed his joy by saying, "Volunteering is the ability to forget your own aches and pains and do something for somebody else without expecting to be paid for it."

Hospitals, churches, local libraries and schools often need volunteers. Help your parents look around

> *"Volunteering is the ability to forget your own aches and pains and do something for somebody else without expecting to be paid for it."*

for other needs and you may both be pleasantly surprised to find new avenues of service.

Ten years ago the National Exchange Club Foundation for the Prevention of Child Abuse was formed in an effort to help stressed parents who were guilty of child abuse. Volunteers were trained by the Foundation to work with stressed families. The project met with great success. Currently there are forty-nine Exchange Centers throughout the United States, with more centers being developed. More than 6,000 children have been helped by the 1,700 volunteers, and every year a greater number of stressed-out parents seek the clubs for help.[3]

The unique feature of the Exchange Club Foundation is that at least one-third of their volunteers are over fifty years old. In the beginning there was great concern that the older volunteers might not be able to relate to the young parents. The oldsters were fearful that they would be resented or rejected by the young, stressed-out parents. Despite these concerns the volunteers project has proven to be most successful.

In discussing the project, Michaele Houston, executive director of the Portland, Oregon Center club, praised the contributions of the older volunteers by saying, "People over fifty are a better match because they aren't threatening. And the children get surrogate grandparents."[4]

School Days

We have all read newspaper accounts of the sixty-five-plus-year-old who has gone back to school and earned a first or an advanced degree. According to a report by the Special Committee on Aging of the United States Senate, there are well over a million persons sixty-five and older who are currently enrolled in some form of higher education.

Many elderly people were unable to continue their education in their younger years for various reasons. Most still regret the missed opportunity. If you have frequently heard—or are still hearing—your parents talk about their lack of educational advantages, maybe now is the time to remedy the situation. It could be that all they need is a little encouragement and reassurance from you to counteract the thought that "It's silly for an old person like me to go back to school." If they are apprehensive about their learning ability, discuss the matter with them. Assure them that an older person's memory and ability may be a bit slower, but learning is possible at all ages.

Colleges and universities are beginning to look to the older generations because many of the baby-boomers are dropping out for various reasons. Courses for older people are unlimited. Almost all institutions of higher learning offer extension courses for continuing education.

If the thought of college and university is too overwhelming, don't overlook the local YMCA, the libraries, or museums that offer lecture series on subjects ranging from art to languages, photography to archaeology. Watch your local newspapers and library bulletin boards for information about courses being offered. Most have reduced prices for senior citizens. And don't overlook the possibility of Bible studies being offered by Bible schools and Bible-teaching churches.

Elderhostel

Once your parents have rediscovered the joy of learning, you may find they are ready for an educational program called *Elderhostel*, which was inspired by the youth hostels of Europe.

Elderhostel is an exciting educational program based on the idea that retirement and later life is a time to enjoy new experiences. It was founded about ten years ago and has been so popular there are now more than 700 institutions participating in all fifty states as well as in foreign countries.

Any person who is sixty or older is eligible to enroll. While the courses are not for credit, they are open to anyone—regardless of whether the participant has earned advanced degrees or has never completed elementary school. Students live in campus dormitories or residential facilities close to classes and dining areas.

The nominal cost (ranging around $200) includes registration, tuition, room and board, use of campus facilities and, often, a variety of extracurricular activities. If financial aid is needed it is often available through a "Hostelship" program. Classes usually extend over a three-week period and include a variety of courses such as history, art, computers, music and more.

For information write to: Elderhostel, 80 Boylston Street, Suite 400, Boston, Massachusetts 02116. A catalogue published three times a year by Elderhostel provides information about the courses offered and where they are taught.

A wonderful way to encourage your parents or to express your confidence in their abilities could be a gift holiday at Elderhostel from the family. If everyone chips in it may not be impossible.

Hobbies

Grandma Moses, America's best-known primitive painter, began her art work by teaching herself to embroider pictures in yarn. At age seventy-six her arthritis was so bad she couldn't continue her needlework. Did that stop her? Not on your life! She found another avenue for her creativity. She started painting. At the age of eighty she gave a one-woman art show in New York City and became famous for her work.

Have you thought of using a hobby as a way of getting an elderly loved one out of the house with a purpose? If, for example, your parents have been taking endless pictures of their grandchildren or dabbling in photography, you may get one of them interested in a photo contest or entering a favorite photo at their local county fair. Watch for these opportunities and find out the requirements for entries. With a bit of encouragement your parent may be off to the library to check out photography magazines or books.

Your mother may enjoy making things with her hands or have a hobby in the field of crafts. Encourage her to contact her church and offer to help with crafts for Vacation Bible School. No doubt she will quickly endear herself to all the staff with her offer.

Nettie has long been known for her green thumb in growing African violets. An alert social worker noticed Nettie's flowers and encouraged her to share her hobby with others in the mobile home park where Nettie lived. As a result Nettie seems to have gained a new lease on life as she became the "expert" among her neighbors.

Part-time Work

Retirement can sometimes be very disappointing for some elderly, especially for the workaholic. To suddenly have a great deal of free time with no real plans of "what to do with the rest of my life" can be frightening and depressing.

Another concern for the able-bodied retirees with little to keep them occupied is learning to live on a "retirement budget" or on a small fixed income. Mounting expenses are not the prescription for a relaxed, leisurely life.

For the persons who have made no plans for retirement, who have no hobbies or other interests and who are living on a small budget, part-time work may be the answer that offers several advantages. First, part-time work gets that retiree out of the house. It uses up part of the leisure time that may have become a curse rather than a blessing, and it provides money to supplement the income. Extra income can mean money for vacations and other luxuries some elderly may otherwise have to forego.

An organization that is a real morale booster and that caters to the older worker (especially to those who may have been eased out of the work force or encouraged to take early retirement) is Operation ABLE (Ability Based on Long Experience). ABLE has offices all across the United States. This organization counsels the applicants and, through interviews, endeavors to link the right ability to the right job.

A word of caution. While part-time work has its advantages, it may also create some problems regarding Social Security. Your parents need to check on their current earning limit. If they do not do so, it is important that you check for them. If they go beyond that earning limit, they will lose some of their present benefits. Monthly benefits are reduced one dollar for every two dollars earned if the income from a part-time job exceeds the limit prescribed by law.

The amount of earning that is permissible changes from time to time. As of May 1988 the limits were $8,400 for persons age sixty-five through sixty-nine, and $6,120 for those under sixty-five. To date, all people seventy years old and older are exempt from earning limits. As an incentive for older people to work, Congress changed the law so that by 1990 benefit reduction will drop to one dollar for every three dollars earned above the limit.[5]

Traveling

Many elderly people are already seasoned travelers as they enjoy the option of taking advantage of their free time to pack and go at every opportunity. However, as our parents become older or after one parent has died, we as adult children sometimes tend to become real worrywarts as we note what we feel to be a decline in their physical conditions. We torture ourselves needlessly as we think of their travels: Mother has never traveled alone—will she get lost? How will Dad manage their luggage with his heart condition? Will they remember to take their medications? What if they get sick? And the more we fret and worry, the greater our fear of imagined disasters!

Does that mean we encourage them to avoid traveling? By no means. If your mother is alone and has not traveled by herself, how about a Christian tour group or cruise? Check out the tour or cruise carefully. Find out as much as you can about the arrangements, accommodations and activities. You may be pleasantly surprised how well your mother can manage in a group of her own peers. And what a morale booster for her when she sees how well she is able to cope!

If there are physical problems, choose the trip carefully, taking into consideration any physical limitations such as back problems or other mild limitations. A recovering heart patient will, of course, not venture on a mountain climbing excursion or explore caves involving numerous steps to climb.

Encourage your parents to talk to their doctor about their pending trip. If it will relieve your anxieties, go to the doctor with them and describe what activities the trip entails. Talk to the doctor about the medication they will need. Secure medical bracelets if they need to wear them. Advise the travel agency of any health problems your parents may have.

If, after you have scrutinized every angle and you still feel worried about having your parents go on a trip, write to The International Association for Medical Assistance to Travelers, 417 Center Street, Lewiston, NY 14092. They have a wealth of tips and suggestions for the older traveler. This is a nonprofit organization and their advertisement suggests you allow six to eight weeks for a response.

Instead of worrying about your parents, why not collect a batch of travel folders featuring tours especially designed for senior citizens? Knowing that you have confidence that they are able to travel can be a real incentive for your parents to venture out on an exciting tour.

Encourage them to take advantage of special discount prices being offered by trains, bus lines, cruise lines and even rental car agencies. Airlines, of course, are well known for their reduced rates for the elderly. Traveling during the week when ordinary travel is lighter can also be a factor in reduced prices. Investigate travel clubs such as the AARP Travel Service, which is exclusively for AARP (American Association of Retired Persons) members, the Silver Wings Plus or the Golden Travelers. Ask your travel agency for other clubs.

If your parents are reasonably healthy, have been checked by their physicians and you have been assured the tour or cruise is paced for the elderly, then stop worrying about them. Why block their plans because of your fears? Commit them to the Lord, bid them bon voyage and let them enjoy their travels while they are able.

Too Soon to Quit!

After reading all the suggestions for involvement, you may be asking: Are these involvement ideas really practical? Do older people really want to be involved once they have retired? People do. At the beginning of this chapter, we hinted at the accumulated wisdom our parents have gained over their lifetime. Why should those talents, that wisdom and those unique abilities be lost when they could be shared with others who desperately need help?

Accounts of all the elderly's accomplishments will never be fully recorded, but let me tell you about just a few persons who fit the psalmist's description and who "still bear fruit in old age."

Fern and Bill were long-time members of a church I attended. After retirement they spent several years in a mission field. Fern, a registered nurse, volunteered her services at the hospital on the mission station. Bill was a carpenter and used his talents and abilities by becoming the all-around handyman. Later, with the help of some of the natives, Bill supervised the building of several homes on the mission compound.

Herman, a retired insurance agent, found great joy and felt useful after he became involved in teaching an adult man how to read. Herman discovered through a literacy program that groups who are in the battle against illiteracy will train tutors (any volunteers) to work one-on-one with learners. Most literacy groups provide a series of workbooks and reading materials. Millions of Americans are functionally illiterate, unable to read and understand a newspaper, write a check, fill out a job application or even apply for Social Security.

For more information you may contact the following sources for the name, address and phone number of the literacy program nearest you: Contact Literacy Center, P.O. Box 81826, Lincoln, NE 68501-1826, phone 800-228-8813; Laubach Literacy Action, Box 131, Syracuse, NY 13210, phone 315-422-9121; and Literacy Volunteers of America, Inc., 5795 Widewaters Parkway, Syracuse, NY 13214, phone 315-455-8000.

When she retired, seventy-year-old Elizabeth was given a beautiful watch from the savings and loan offices as a token of appreciation for her long years of excellent service. Just as the first newness of retirement was beginning to wear thin, she received a phone call from Pat, a fellow church member and a harried caregiver. Pat's mother, Maude, was very concerned about her own finances and had trouble balancing her checkbook. Maude called Pat at least once or twice a week wanting help with her account. Pat functioned on a very tight schedule. Not only did she work part-time, she had her own family and her mother-in-law to care for. In desperation Pat called Elizabeth for help.

Elizabeth gladly helped Maude balance her checkbook. Being the well-organized accountant that she was, Elizabeth also sent a simple but clear statement to Maude about every three weeks so that Maude could *see* exactly how much money she had in her accounts.

Maude was so pleased and the system worked so well that Elizabeth soon found herself busy putting her knowledge to work by keeping the accounts of several widows in the church who had heard about Maude's good find. These widows had always depended on their husbands to handle the family finances, and they were uneasy and fearful about their accounts. Not only did Elizabeth feel needed by using her abilities, but several worried widows felt better knowing someone was available for guidance and to answer questions.

Frank, an avid reader, used his extra leisure time

to delve into the Scriptures. The result was that despite his advancing years he became one of the most popular Bible teachers in the adult Sunday School department of his church.

Opportunities for senior citizens to stay involved are many. You as an adult child may make your suggestions and then give your parents the right to choose what they will do to remain active instead of withdrawing from life. For any able-bodied person, it really is too soon to quit!

Notes

1. Psalm 92:14, italics added
2. Harold B. Smith, "Beyond Sun City" (editorial), *Christianity Today*, February 19, 1988.
3. Upfront, "Bringing Help to Troubled Families," *Modern Maturity* magazine, Vol. 32, February-March, 1989.
4. Ibid.
5. *NRTA News Bulletin*, "A Disincentive to Stay on the Job." Washington, D.C., May 1988, Vol. 29, No. 5, p.11.

Chapter Four
Games Older People Play

To avoid any false concept, let me quickly clarify that playing games is not limited to any specific age group. At times all of us, regardless of age, have been guilty of indulging in games. Game playing often gets sprinkled into our efforts to communicate and to display acceptable behavior. We know what is expected of us in order to be considered well mannered and socially acceptable, so we fall into the trap of game playing. Let me give you several scenarios to make sure we are on the same wave length as we begin to consider playing games.

All week thirty-five-year-old Gloria had been looking forward to this night out with the girls. Now greetings and chatter fill the room. They are a happy group and truly good friends—or so it would appear. Let's listen carefully and see what is *really* going on.

"Hi, Pam! You look great!" (*She really is beginning to show her age. Why doesn't she do something about that mousy hair?*)

"What a perfectly stunning outfit, Jan!" (*Makes her*

look at least ten pounds heavier and she can't afford that.)

"The kids? Oh, Jim's with them. He encourages me to go out." (*Especially after our brawl tonight. He's probably climbing the walls by now!*)

***

Lest you men may feel a bit smug because the spotlight in the above scenario is focused on a group of women, how about this?

After dinner Jack is in the den sprawled out in his favorite LazyBoy, buried in the sports page. Then he hears his wife say, "Look what I found while on my lunch hour today."

Jack slowly lowers the newspaper as she models her latest bargain. He hates the color and the style —and it definitely looks too expensive to be much of a bargain!

"Do you like it, Honey?" she asks.

Despite all the mental negatives flashing through his mind, Jack replies, "It's great, Hon. You look terrific."

***

Did your children ever pretend to be sick in order to stay home from school and avoid an assignment they failed to prepare for? Or perhaps they felt slightly neglected so they pretended an ailment. Often it worked. They received the extra attention they were striving to get. Bringing the question closer to home, have *you* ever called in sick in an attempt to avoid a knotty problem at work?

What adult has not been guilty of bending over backward to please the boss, to laugh loudly at his

jokes and to try to put on a facade of interest while listening to one of his more boring lectures? If we are
realistic we need to admit that we all know how to
change our behavior in order to manipulate, to
exploit, to use or even to control others. Habits are
formed early in life and psychologists tell us our inter-
action and behavior are often determined by the
behavior of our parents.

---

*Personalities...do not change
just because one has reached a ripe
old age....The self-centered perfectionist becomes even more
demanding with age.*

Family counselor Dr. Judith Alexandre agrees that
playing games is not limited to children or even to
adult children. She indicated that personalities per se
do not change just because one has reached the ripe
old age of seventy or eighty. The self-centered,
demanding perfectionist becomes even more demanding with age.

Sometimes we mellow as we age because we have
reassessed our values. What was vitally important at
one stage of our lives sometimes becomes less important as the years slip by. However, our basic perspec-
tive or world-view, says Dr. Alexandre, remains some-

what the same. Our personhood doesn't change nor do the games we play. The difference for adult children is that they are now in the unfamiliar role of observing, experiencing and trying to understand the games played by elderly parents.

Games Older People Play

This chapter is not an attempt to put down elderly people or to in any way destroy the proper role and respect that should exist between adult children and their parents. I am a firm believer in the dignity of the individual and in obeying the biblical command to honor one's parents. However, by examining some of the common games families play, adult children may better be able to understand the problems confronting them.

We have established the fact that playing games is a trait of human nature. Older people who have had years of practice often become more skillful at game-playing than the younger generation. Most older parents know *exactly* what games work best with each of their children to obtain the desired results. From experience many adult children recognize their parents' games, but that does not mean the children always come out the winners when involved in some of the following games.

"If You Really Loved Me!"

A game in which all of us can easily become involved is the game of manipulation. The scenario changes to fit the age and circumstances of the players.

Despite her seventy-six years Mabel maintained her own home and, for the most part, was quite independent. Frequently, when she felt neglected or when it was to her advantage, that independence disappeared rapidly. Her son, Bob, lived in a city about a hundred miles away. Mabel received regular phone calls from Bob, plus letters—well, the letters were mostly from Sue, Bob's wife, because Bob hates to write letters.

Mabel often complained because Bob didn't write. Sue patiently but kindly explained how busy they were. Bob was usually tied up with a business deal that demanded long hours.

On one occasion when Mabel called her son's home only to find Bob out on a business trip, Sue tried to encourage her mother-in-law. Sue complimented Mabel on how well she was managing on her own and how much they appreciated her help. Then Sue said, "You know, Mabel, *my* mother is ill right now. By trying to visit her as often as possible, keeping Dad happy and tending to the needs of Bob and the kids, I'm really swamped."

Sue's efforts, however, failed. Within a few days Mabel called again and demanded to speak to Bob. At the sound of his voice, she described what she felt was a crisis that needed Bob's immediate attention. Her furnace had been giving her trouble and needed to be replaced, but she was afraid to buy a new one without Bob's help. Bob tried to reassure his mother and then he suggested a friend whom they both knew who would be glad to help her select a new furnace to meet her needs. Mabel would not be put off. She began to cry and indicated she had not been well, insisting that Bob come to see her. Mabel won that game. Bob dropped everything and rushed to see his mother, who felt fine once he arrived.

Bob and Sue recalled that this wasn't the first time Mabel had a "crisis." In the summer, when she discovered that Bob and his family were planning a vacation in Hawaii instead of their annual visit to her home, another crisis threatened to erupt. Bob suggested that while they were in Hawaii Mabel visit her sister in a nearby state. He would send her a roundtrip plane ticket for the two hour flight. Mabel insisted she wasn't well enough to travel. With a deep sigh she informed Bob that she would try to manage on her own despite her illness. She would just remain at home "while you enjoy yourselves." The Hawaiian trip was far from relaxing. Bob was torn between his "felt" obligation to his mother and the obligation to his wife and family.

Older people who attempt to manipulate their children as Mabel did often do so out of fear that they are being put aside and forgotten. They worry about what will happen to them if they become ill while their children are not close by. No doubt jealousy was a factor when Mabel learned how much time Sue was spending with her own parents. Basically, manipulation is an attempt for reassurance and a cry for more attention because the elderly want more of their children's time.

In evaluating Bob's response to his mother, it is obvious that Mabel was successful in controlling his life. In both cases Bob attempted to break free by offering an alternative. By suggesting a solution to the furnace problem and an alternative vacation trip, Bob gave his mother the privilege of choosing a way out of her problem. Unfortunately, Mabel knew how she could break down her son and she did. While it is never easy for most of us to oppose our parents, Bob might have gained greater control of the situation by kindly but firmly saying something like, "Mother, I love you. I know you want me to spend more time with you and I want to be with you. However, right now I cannot leave and come to see you. For now this is the best I can do." He could then have proceeded with the responsibilities to his work and to his wife and children.

"Poor Little Ol' Me!"

This is a game of self-put-downs. The game is, in fact, another form of the manipulation game. The players tend to use the ravages of old age or the natural results of the aging process to exploit the younger generation by means of a put-down of self. The put-downs may range from their own inabilities resulting from age to their personal appearance.

Joan and her mother, Betty, are an excellent example of this game. Joan finally sought professional help because she was so frustrated by her mother's attitude and actions.

In her youth seventy-five-year-old Betty won a college beauty contest. After her marriage Betty was still known in her hometown as the most beautiful and best-dressed woman around. She was a prominent leader in local society for years. When advancing years began to rob Betty of some of that beauty, her personality seemed to change also. And Betty began to use her fading beauty as a way of putting herself down, much to the confusion of her children and grandchildren. When Betty's family invited her to join them for an event or activity, her standard response was something to the effect, "Oh, you don't want an old, ugly woman like me tagging along."

At first her grandchildren were surprised and

quickly assured Betty that they did want her to go with them. Eventually, however, both the children and grandchildren tired of Betty's game. Joan said, "My kids don't even want me to invite their grandmother anymore. When I do and they hear her response, they are very slow in assuring her that we invited her because we *do* want her. Their hesitation causes Mother to feel hurt, and we have a big argument as I try to reassure her."

Betty frequently compared herself with her peers as she talked to Joan, with comments like, "I look much older than Fran, don't I?" or "Ruby is more fun to have around than I am."

In talking about the problem, Joan admitted her frustration. "Over and over I asked myself, 'Why does she do that?' We tell her again and again that we love her, that we want her with us and that we think she is beautiful. Why is she so vain? Perhaps I don't understand because I was never beautiful."

From a professional counselor Joan learned that vanity is not the real culprit for her mother and other older people who play the game of putting themselves down. Part of the problem is their inability to accept the natural bodily deterioration that comes with age. As these people see the brown spots on their hands, the wrinkles in their faces and the flabby arm muscles, they push the panic button. They cry for sympathy and assurance. They have always depended on their attractiveness, their special talents or abilities and their charming personalities to help them get ahead. Now, as these assets are disappearing, they cannot believe they can be accepted for the people they are. Because they have not successfully dealt with the aging process and accepted it, they belittle themselves in a plea for acceptance and in an attempt to avoid expected rejection.

"This Is the Big One!"

The third game was excellently demonstrated in a TV sitcom, popular some years ago, entitled "Sanford and Son." Sanford, the elderly man played by actor Redd Foxx, tried to control his son and any situation that was not to his liking by faking a heart attack. Clutching his chest he would insist, "This is the big one!"

There are hypochondriacs in every age group who attempt to use real or imagined ailments to an advantage. A forty-year-old claimed to have a "problem knee" and, in the presence of his co-workers, sought sympathy by painstakingly hauling himself up the stairs one step at a time. One day—apparently thinking no one was watching—I saw him taking two steps at a time as he ran up the stairs. When I later asked him about his knee, he began telling me about the pain he constantly suffered with it.

As Dr. Judith Alexandre said, game playing does not stop because a person reaches a certain age. By magnifying their infirmities, older people vie for sympathy and control. For example, if Grandpa is living in your home, your teenagers cannot have their friends in or play their loud music after eight o'clock because Grandpa goes to bed early. Teenagers and their music upset him. True, he is hard of hearing—that is, until you discuss family matters in which you would prefer he weren't involved—but he insists he can hear the teen's music "blaring away."

Bertha, a retired school teacher, recently moved next door to her son and his family. She depends solely on her children for fellowship because she is new in the neighborhood, but her main complaint is that no one takes time to talk to her.

Her children are sympathetic but they complain that it is difficult to find any subject of mutual interest to discuss because Bertha has withdrawn from life. When her family suggests books and magazines that might interest her, she insists that "my eyes are gone." Instead, she spends her day watching soaps on TV. When the family mentioned to Bertha that they had heard about a nearby Day Care Center that needed available grandparents to help out a few hours each week, Bertha insisted she had "already put in my time with children" and was now too nervous to be around youngsters.

Bertha has no major health problems. She has a pleasant home but she wallows in self-pity and loneliness. She is taking advantage of her age and the usual infirmities. To gain sympathy and attention, her favorite clincher is, "The day will come when I'll be out of your way and you won't need to be bothered with me anymore." With that she attempts to lay a guilt trip on her family, and she is often successful.

Most counselors agree that, when parents have received the best care and attention the family is able to give, guilt must not be permitted to erode the lives of adult children and their offspring. Despite imagined claims of neglect from lonely parents, the adult child must not sacrifice his or her own family and responsibilities.

"You Won't Get a Dime!"

A fourth game older people resort to is the money game. There are actually two sides to this game. One side is played by the well-to-do, though not necessarily wealthy, parent who uses money to control the family. Persons who were fortunate enough to gain some wealth during their lifetime often look upon the younger generation with contempt. Clutching their money, they resent thinking of giving an inheritance to the "undeserving younger generation."

These elderly feel their children are just waiting, like the proverbial vultures, to get their hands on the inheritance that will soon be theirs. Unfortunately, there *are* some children who are guilty of this, but not most. The oldsters who use money as power to gain control threaten to write out of the will any undeserving hopefuls who fail to comply with the elderly's wishes—bizarre though they may be.

The other side of the money game involves a certain amount of pride because most of the elderly have a sincere longing to leave a handsome inheritance for their children. Middle-class and poorer people have a constant fear that they will run out of money. With soaring prices in our day, who can fail to understand that fear? To these elderly a lack of money is of deep concern because it could mean they will become financially dependent upon their children, and no parent wants to be a burden.

You may find it difficult to understand your parents when they do not want to move to a semi-care or complete-care facility, despite the fact that they should. You feel they could afford to do so but they insist they can manage in their own home. However, you are spending more time than ever as you stop at their home daily to check on them. The evidence you find of their need for supervision on each of your visits is far from reassuring. Nevertheless, they are firm on their decision for independence. If hard pressed you would find that their reasoning would be something like this: "If we move into a place where we will receive help, it will be costly. What if we get sick and run up bills? Maybe we won't have enough money." Even if the money stretches to cover their own expenses, their concern is still your inheritance. Their heart's cry is, "Our money will be gone and our children won't get a dime!" To many elderly, that fact spells failure.

Do We Stop the Games?

We cannot stop the games but perhaps we can make some changes. Habits that have been firmly established in people over a long period of time are difficult to break. And people who have for years perfected their skills at playing certain games will not suddenly change. However, with patience, love and prayer, some attitudes and perspectives can be slightly shifted slightly toward improvement as we gain new insights into a situation. One important step in gaining new insights is good communication.

Many adult children are frustrated when they try to talk with their parents because neither parents nor children have ever learned how to listen. Yet listening is the crucial requirement for good communication. Too frequently talks between adult children and their parents dwindle down to nothing more than complaints and sniping at one another, and that is not communication. In desperation, therefore, both parties decide that talking to each other is impossible.

When you reach a deadlock with your parents, try talking less and listening more. That is not easy, but it is possible to learn to listen and to improve listening skills. One technique to improve communication and to give the elderly an opportunity to be heard is to repeat back to them in your own words what they are saying. That technique forces you to listen carefully, rather than preparing your next argument. Often, when our parents feel they are being heard and under-

We dare not...overlook the fundamental truth that each person, regardless of age,...is an individual with his or her own dignity and pride.

stood, they in turn are more ready to hear our suggested solution to the problem at hand.

Another good communication technique is to slow down. The thinking pattern of the elderly is not as quick as it once was. If you discuss a problem by talking "top speed" and insist that the older person give you an immediate answer or decision, you have just destroyed any possibility for communicating. An elderly person will usually respond by becoming frustrated, confused and angry. He or she will realize the impossibility of keeping up and become discouraged as self-confidence begins to melt away. Gerontologists tell us that an elderly person's thinking and speaking patterns are very similar. Listen to your parent speak and adjust your speaking pace accordingly.

Your attempt at better communication may be a bit strained at first, and you and your parent may slip back to some of the old patterns. But you may both be pleasantly surprised at some of the problem-solutions you find when the two of you learn to really communicate—and all of that without the aid of playing games!

The Armchair Psychologist

As I conclude this chapter I am reminded of one of my psychology professors who loved to taunt his students by saying, "There is nothing more dangerous than an armchair psychologist!" And, of course, he was correct. The games mentioned in this chapter are only a few of the most common, and they are just that—games. We need to remember that elderly people are prone to numerous diseases, some of which may affect their mental capacities. Any behavioral changes observed in an elderly person must definitely be referred to a medical professional for diagnosis. Under no circumstance should an unusual or strange behavior be attributed to being "just a game he or she is playing."

Often the actions, attitudes and games older people play are difficult for us to cope with or even to understand. We dare not, however, overlook the fundamental truth that each person, regardless of age or position in life, is an individual with his or her own dignity and pride. When we fail to recognize that truth, we create problems for them as well as for ourselves. My mother had a favorite verse from the

Psalms, which she quoted frequently and which made me realize her own personal dependence upon her Lord: "I was young and now I am old, yet I have never seen the righteous forsaken."[1] Somehow the Lord always saw us through each difficult situation.

Note

1. Psalm 37:25

Chapter Five
Options for Living Arrangements

After his father died, Ray worried about his mother, Lottie, living alone. He and his wife, Mildred, begged Lottie to come and live with them but she declined. "I'm fine, Ray," she said. "Now stop worrying about me!"

Lottie felt she was in good health and she didn't want to intrude on her son and his family. She insisted on her independence. "I live close enough so I can run in to see you and the grandchildren," she told Ray and Mildred. "I have my friends and the church. Of course, I miss your dad more than you'll ever know, but I'll get along. Let me enjoy my independence while I can." Ray and Mildred wisely respected Lottie's wishes because she was so confident and appeared to be doing okay.

One day, however, Lottie's independence was quickly snatched from her when she had a severe stroke that left her badly paralyzed. Suddenly she went from being a vibrant, independent, grand lady to a confused, helpless patient who needed twenty-four-hour care.

Lottie's situation is not unusual. An elderly person may move along through the years functioning reasonably well, insisting on independence and presenting few if any problems to the children. But one day, as with Lottie, a crisis occurs and the family is thrust into a position of needing outside assistance at once.

What Are the Options?

Fortunately, crises do not invade the lives of all elderly in an identical pattern. Many will continue to live independently all their lives. Others may need to find smaller, maintenance-free housing to fit failing abilities and a tighter economical budget. Some may need more and more assistance with personal and household tasks in order to remain in their own homes. A widely accepted statistic indicates that only 5 percent of the elderly population over sixty-five will eventually need the complete, supervised care offered by a convalescent hospital or nursing home. (Statisticians realize that 5 percent is not a final figure. As life expectancy continues to increase, the need for extended care is expected to slowly increase also.)

Contrary to popular belief, older people *do* have a choice in where they live. The problem is that many elderly and their families are not aware of the choices available in living arrangements, care and services. Too many elderly fear that if they become ill or disabled or even if they admit to slowing down a bit, a nursing home is the next step because it is the only possible source of help. Not so! In this chapter we will list some of the options available to provide the older person with living arrangements to meet individual needs and preferences.

Their Own Homes

Most older people prefer living in their own homes rather than living with their children, even after the loss of a spouse. This preference is confirmed by a report from the National Center for Health, which indicates that 80 percent of those living alone are women. Most gerontologists agree that independent living should be encouraged as long as the elderly can safely manage on their own.

Older people experience a feeling of security in their own homes and, unless property taxes have skyrocketed to an impossible level, the old home is most likely the least expensive housing available. Because many elderly have lived in their home for years, it is filled with memories and ties that are heartrending to sever. Unless the neighborhood has changed immensely, your parents are surrounded by neighbors and friends they have known for years. In most cases their favorite doctor, dentist and shopping center are all conveniently located and easily accessible. All of these factors contribute to a feeling of contentment.

In their own homes the elderly have their own set pattern for their daily routines so that, when it becomes necessary for you to step in to help or just to check on your parent, it is very important that you not take over and insist that *your* routine or life-style must be followed. Whether or not you agree with your parent, it is vital that you allow that person the dignity of his or her own personal routine, standards or personal values.

Condominiums

In time the housing situation for your parents may change. Physical conditions of one or both parents may prohibit climbing stairs. This could result in a need to move from a home with several floors to a one-floor home. If the neighborhood has deteriorated to the extent of being dangerous, the house too large or in need of huge repairs, a change may be wise. Or even if the yard work or general upkeep of the home becomes a burden, your parents may suggest—or, at least, consider—selling their home and moving into smaller quarters.

Most adults resent change, and that resentment often increases with age. The elderly should not be rushed into a move. A decision of this nature takes time. Whether your parents choose their new living arrangements, whether you are involved in the decision or whether the responsibility becomes entirely yours, the decision for housing should be made carefully and thoughtfully.

The familiar adage is still true: A man's home is his castle. Next to their health, housing is probably the most important factor in the life of elderly people—especially since a great percentage of time is spent at home after retirement. Every person is entitled to a decent, safe, comfortable place to live. It was the fifteenth-century Spanish writer Miguel Saavedra de Cervantes who said it best: "You are a king by your own fireside, as much as any monarch on his throne."

If your parents are physically able to manage on their own, they may consider living quarters that allow independent living without having the responsibility of a lot of upkeep. If so, a condominium may be the answer.

Investing their capital gain from the sale of their home in the purchase of a condo would give them the freedom of ownership as well as tax benefits homeowners enjoy. There is, however, a monthly maintenance fee. Make sure your parents understand that the maintenance fee is based on the size, floor plan and location of each unit.

They also need to understand that a condo board, elected by the owners, may hire professional maintenance persons to care for the building and grounds. If your parents are interested in gardening and caring for flowers, they will be pleased to know that many condos have small areas for owners interested in that activity to do so.

Moving into smaller living quarters means disposing of some of the possessions your parents have collected for years. Parting with their treasures is not easy and your parents need your understanding and support. Put yourself into their shoes. You will no doubt agree that one doesn't realize how precious one's possessions are until it is time to part with them. If your mother is sentimental—and most women are—every item with which she must part will no doubt have a meaningful memory associated with it. This does not mean, however, that they keep everything. They can't. Space is limited in smaller quarters. But you can be understanding and realize that, although they must dispose of things that may seem useless to you, giving away those items may cause your parents a lot of pain.

Cooperative Housing

Cooperative housing was the choice for Bill and JoAnne who, at retirement, were tired of the upkeep and the yard work required in the home they had owned for years. Now that the children were gone,

Bill and JoAnne sold their home and bought into a cooperative housing project. Bill, in speaking of their new home, said, "We really like it. It's less work and taxes are quite a bit lower than we paid on our old home. Who wouldn't go for that? We're even able to save on our grocery bills. They have what they call 'co-op buying' and all the tenants get together to buy groceries in bulk—not bad!"

Cooperative housing is different from purchasing a condo. Cooperative housing is just that—cooperative. Buyers chip in and buy the entire unit together. Each owner is then entitled to live in a particular unit. The reason taxes are often lower is because, unlike a private home, the tax assessment is made on the entire cooperative housing project rather than on each individual living unit. While there are monthly occupancy fees, many people like Bill and JoAnne feel they have a greater share of control than in a condo because they have a share in the entire project rather than in just one unit.

Mobile Homes

A very popular, affordable housing possibility—especially in Southern California—is a mobile home. That popularity is spreading rapidly. The American Association of Retired Persons (AARP) reports that one out of every three homes sold in the United States is a mobile-manufactured home. It requires less maintenance than the large, traditional, rambling or two-story home. Before you skip over the next paragraphs, insisting that a mobile *is not* for *your* parents, you may want to take a second look.

Mobile homes today are far different from the narrow, scruffy trailers of the past that were usually found in the poor section of a city. Mobile homes are now often built to owner specifications for floor plan and color scheme. Many have two to three bedrooms, two baths, with porches and patios. Mobile home parks are usually neat and attractive with well-groomed yards and streets.

The advantages of mobile home living, in addition to requiring less maintenance, is that the initial purchase price is less than a private home (although prices continue to rise). In some mobile home parks the land may be purchased, as well as the home. In other parks the tenant pays a monthly space rent, but since mobile homes are considered personal property and not real estate, there is a tax advantage. Many parks are for adults only and most have small yards for flowers, trees and gardens.

Apartments

If your parents are not interested in or able to own any of the housing possibilities suggested above, they may want to consider renting their own apartment. That way, when the water heater needs to be replaced or the air conditioner malfunctions, it is the landlord's problem. There is freedom in apartment living in that, when your parents want to take a vacation, they can lock the door and take off.

An important consideration in apartment living is the problem of the tremendous rent increases in some areas. Since a rent increase can create a problem for people on a limited budget, a "senior apartment" may be the answer.

Senior apartments are specifically designed to

meet the needs and preferences of older people on fixed incomes. These apartments are usually equipped with small kitchenettes for the purpose of getting breakfast or snacks, but the main meal is served in a central dining facility. This meal service (if available) is a plus because it provides a nutritious, low-cost meal. Social workers have found that poor appetites of elderly persons who eat alone are often stimulated as they eat in a group setting with their peers.

Senior apartments are often co-sponsored by the government and the American Association of Homes for the Aging (AAHA). AAHA affiliated state associations can be found in thirty-seven states around the country. They have answers to many questions concerning senior housing as well as elderly care questions. For more information look in your phone book for the AAHA association in your area or write to: American Association of Homes for the Aging, 1129 20th Street, N.W., Suite 400, Washington, D.C., 20036, phone 202-296-5960. Ask for free brochures available from AAHA. Be sure to send a self-addressed, stamped, business-sized envelope to the above address.

A Two-Generation Family

A knotty question that frequently confronts a family who is considering housing options for elderly parents is: Should we have Mother (or Dad) move in with us? Before you immediately assume a positive answer, you need to consider a number of questions very carefully.

For many adult children to even consider any other option means they are overwhelmed with guilt. But do you realize that national surveys reveal that the *majority* of adults in the United States think it is a bad idea for elderly parents to move in with their children? The interesting fact is that this is the consensus of both the younger as well as the older people. Older people especially do not want to become a burden to their children. Undoubtedly, that is the reason so many elderly have vowed never, under any circumstances, to live with their children.

Most experts feel that moving a parent into your home with your family should be a last resort.

If you are seriously considering having a parent move into your home, you need to review the following questions very carefully:

1. How do your spouse and/or children feel about the move?
2. Do you have room for another occupant in your home without cramping your own family?
3. How will this move affect your family budget? Will you be the sole financial supporter?
4. How will the necessary medical expenses for your parent be met?
5. What about your parent's social needs? Will you and your family be the only source of companionship and entertainment?

6. Will the move take your parent away from his or her own church? If so, how will you supplement this need for Christian fellowship?

7. How well do you get along with your parent? Do you clash? Will your parent constantly voice an opinion on running your home and/or rearing your children?

8. How will this move *really* affect you, your spouse and your children? It's their home, too, that you are opening to another occupant. How will this move affect the privacy of your own immediate family?

9. Is it wise to replace the familiar surroundings of your parent's home with a home that is buzzing with activity?

10. Would your parent really feel at home? Do you honestly think the move into your home is the best living option for your parent?[1]

Set aside a time for every member of your family to frankly discuss these questions if you are, in fact, toying with the idea of having your parent move into your home. Give your parent a copy of the questions and encourage him or her to respond honestly to each one. Spend time in prayer as you consider all the ramifications of this move, and above all be open to God's guidance. It is far better to avoid a crisis of a wrong decision than to move blindly and eventually find yourself in a situation that everyone will regret. Most experts feel that moving a parent into your home with your family should be a last resort.

Home Safety

If your parents are living independently and are at the stage where they only need help now and then, you need to make sure their home is as safe as possible. Insurance companies report that one of the most common causes of injuries and death in our country are accidents in the home. This fact becomes even more pronounced and dangerous for the older people whose bodies are not as spry as they once were.

The following safety checks for your parents' home are suggested in a book published by AARP:

1. Check for sufficient light inside and out.
2. Make sure all electrical cords are in good condition.
3. Install night-lights in bedroom, bath and halls.
4. Remove scatter rugs or be sure rugs are skid-proof.
5. Install hand rails and ramps where necessary.
6. Check hot-water heater and set at 110 degrees or lower to avoid burn accidents.
7. Install nonskid strips and grab bars in tub and shower. Place grab bar next to toilet also.
8. Print emergency telephone number in large numbers next to every phone.
9. Install smoke detectors at crucial areas in the home and check sprinkler system.
10. Check furnace and exhaust systems and replace filters regularly.
11. Check locks on doors and windows.
12. Check for needed repairs and take care of them.[2]

Kitchen Safety

An area of your parents' home that needs to be carefully and consistently examined for safety is the kitchen. Shopping and preparing food often becomes too much of an effort, especially if the elderly person lives alone. When you visit your parent, watch for any signs that indicate a lack of proper nutritional food and fluid intake. Watch, also, for food spills or water leaks on the floor that could cause the elderly to fall. Without making an issue of it, try to inconspicuously look for dirty pans, dishes and silverware that failing eyesight may have overlooked when doing the dishes.

If your parents, like mine, lived through the Depression, you know that throwing out food is almost comparable to committing a sin! Tight budgets often contribute to saving leftovers too long. Added to that problem is their fading sense of smell, taste and sight, all of which means the oldster could become ill if the food has been stored improperly or so long that it has become moldy or spoiled.

Shirley Peterson, County home adviser for the University of California, listed a number of helpful suggestions in the *Ventura County Star-Free Press* concerning kitchen safety for the elderly. You, the adult child, need to check the refrigerator and clear out leftovers at least every other week. Peterson suggests that you move older packaged frozen food to the front of the freezer before placing newly wrapped food behind the older packages. Each parcel should be clearly labeled and dated in large, bold letters. By taking your parent shopping (or doing the shopping yourself) you make sure that a variety of food groups are purchased, such as dairy, meats, fish, grains, vegetables and soft fruits such as bananas, grapes or pears.

To be sure your parent is eating properly, why not prepare several batches of food and then package them like commercial TV dinners, which need only to be reheated. A portable oven timer can be set when the older cook places the food into the oven to remind him or her to check food when hot.

Shirley Peterson also suggests we encourage the elderly to use a microwave to prepare tea or coffee. When a hot drink can be prepared easily and quickly, the elderly may consume more needed fluids.[3]

Many gadgets and other helpful tools are available to assist the elderly who lack dexterity or hand strength. Contact your local or state social service agency, local supportive services for the elderly or local home health agency for information on gadgets such as jar openers, cap poppers, reachers for items on a top shelf or gripper pads.

Telephone Reassurance

While making your parents' living quarters as comfortable and safe as possible, don't overlook the added safety provided by the telephone. We are all quick to agree that the elderly, especially those who live alone, must have a telephone. However, what if they cannot get to the phone to call for help due to an accident or illness?

Many adult children devise a system of checking on their parents by calling at the same time every day. Some older people set up their own buddy system in which several elderly friends call each other and check in that way.

There are different volunteer commercial phone-checking services available for a moderate fee. The local police departments in some areas offer phone reassurance services. Either the elderly will call the service at a specific time(s), or the service will call the elderly. If the older person does not call in or does not respond when called, help is immediately sent to the home. If there is no answer at the door, the police or local firemen will check further and enter if necessary. This service is well worth the small fee involved because lives have been saved by it.

A paging system that is most helpful is also available. The older person wears or carries an instrument that is electronically connected to a central dispatcher.

There is such a difference in the aging process, we cannot set a specific age and say: When your parent reaches seventy-five he or she is no longer able to live alone.

If your parent falls, has a heart attack or stroke, or needs any sort of help, the dispatcher receives a signal and calls to discover the problem. If the elderly does not answer the phone, the dispatcher sends emergency assistance to the home immediately.

Call your local American Association for the Aging office, the local police or telephone company to find out about the telephone reassurance service in your area. Or to secure a booklet entitled "Service for Special Needs," contact: The New York Telephone Company's Communication Center for Disabled Customers, 1095 Avenue of the Americas, New York, NY 10036.

Outside Help Available

We are usually so closely involved with our parents it is sometimes difficult to know when they need more help than they are presently receiving. Because there is such a difference in the aging process, we cannot set a specific age and say: When your parent reaches seventy-five, for instance, he or she is no longer able to live alone.

Most parents want to maintain their independence as long as possible. They don't want to become a burden to their families; therefore, their pride often prevents them from admitting their need or asking for additional help when they really need it. What, then, can an adult child do in order not to neglect parents but still avoid becoming overprotective? Let's look at some of the help available outside your parents' home.

Case/Social Workers

One excellent source of assistance for the elderly can come from social workers found in such service organizations as the Administration on Aging, your County Agency on Aging, some hospitals and family service agencies. Social workers are well versed in the needs of the elderly and are able to evaluate physical, social and psychological needs of your parents. After assessing their needs and their situation, many social workers are ready to give you further guidance by suggesting other services your parents may need, as well as how and where to obtain these services.

With the growing demand for assessment services, many private firms have been established in recent years. While their fees are often on a sliding scale, the private firms are in the service to make a profit. If you contact a privately owned agency for assessment, be sure to inquire about the financial rates. Some adult children have been surprised to discover that firms such as these may have a price range of $45 to $85 an hour for assessment.

Home Delivered Meals

You or the social worker may notice that your parent is not eating properly. Because good nutrition is vital for the total health of the elderly, you may want to contact some of the many agencies, as well as some church organizations, to discover what home delivered meals are available in the area.

One nutrition program is called Home Delivered Meals. Since this is a federally funded program, it cannot charge for the hot meals it offers, although some suggest a donation from the family.

Another very popular meal program is Meals on Wheels. In some areas this program is supported entirely by private donations; in other areas the federal government contracts with local agencies. Meals on Wheels is then supported by private, community and federal funds, with the fee on a sliding scale.

Usually the elderly may order two meals a day from Meals on Wheels. Consideration is given to the receiver who may have special dietary or dental problems.

Because of the various sponsors for meal programs across the land, there is also a variation in fees. Nevertheless, these food programs are a helpful highlight to many lonely senior citizens. Eighty-plus-year-old Ed, my next door neighbor, lives alone with his black and white cat, Bootsie, despite several strokes and a heart attack. With his lopsided grin, Ed insists he looks forward to noontimes. The food Meals on Wheels delivers daily is excellent, and the volunteers are so friendly. What could be more important than a hot, delicious meal and a friendly contact from the outside world!

Visiting Nurse Association

When parents who are living independently in their own homes become ill, suffer from a chronic illness, or return home after a hospital stay, many adult children panic. Who will care for the elderly until they can manage on their own again? The answer for assistance can be found in the Visiting Nurse Association (VNA), in existence for more than a hundred years, with local chapters in most areas. VNA has been, and still is, the answer to the prayers of many adult children, most of whom have nothing but praise for VNA.

Visiting Nurse Association offers services at reduced cost and, in some cases, at no cost at all. The chapters are usually operated by volunteer organizations, which explains their sliding scale of fees. Sometimes, *but not always*, their services are covered by Medicaid/Medicare programs.

VNA staff is made up of registered nurses, public health nurses and licensed practical nurses. In addition to the professionals there are also elderly volunteers who want to remain active. The elderly volunteers are usually assigned to respite care duty, which means being assigned to a specific family to sit with a home-bound person while an exhausted caregiver takes an hour or an afternoon off to do necessary errands or just to have a short time out.

Services of the professional nurse—usually

referred to the patient by a physican—include caring for all physical needs, such as bathing, feeding, changing dressings, dispensing medications, toilet needs and shaving. Often the nurses also teach families how to make life easier for themselves, as well as the patient. Depending on the circumstances the nurse may come to the home every day or several times a week for a short visit.

Senior Centers

Functions of senior centers have expanded greatly since they were first established. Their main purpose at one time was to provide social activities for the elderly, while the objectives in many centers today include a program that offers a much wider selection of activities. Some centers have excellent social workers who plan outings and classes in a variety of subjects for the elderly. Others offer counseling and give home health care tips. Still other centers provide transportation and escort services, and some even provide hot meals—these àre over and above any other hot meal program the elderly may already have.

Senior centers offer an opportunity to the semi-home bound elderly to get out and enjoy contacts with the outside world and to fellowship with peers.

To find out about the senior centers in your area, call your city or state Agency on Aging or your local Information and Referral Agency.

Other Services for the Elderly

Many areas have In-Home Support Services (IHSS). This is a program designed especially for the functionally impaired. It is funded by both the federal and state governments and its services range from household care, personal care, transportation to and from medical appointments, to protective supervision. Any elderly person who is blind or disabled and is in poor economic straits usually qualifies for IHSS services if there is enough evidence that he or she cannot stay at home without the services IHSS offers.

In some cities and states there are escort and transportation services for the elderly, which relieves the busy, overworked adult child from that duty. San Francisco and Los Angeles, for example, have a Senior Escort Outreach Program established by the local police department. Any senior citizen in these areas may call the police department for assistance in getting to the bank, the Medicare office, or for other errands.

It is impossible to list all of the services available. You may find additional assistance by calling your local department of social services or Area Agency on Aging (AAA), listed in your telephone directory. From the information included in this chapter, there can be no doubt that there are indeed many services available that will make the situation as convenient as possible for your aging parents who are living independently in their own homes.

A Word of Caution

In talking with and listening to many adult children involved in caregiving, I have found that many have nothing but praise for the help they received from available agencies and services. However, I also found that other families had—or still have—an unrealistic idea of the help available to them. Many of the latter group, for example, have an ideal but unrealistic concept that the government will step in and provide all the financial aid needed at each level of caregiving. Unfortunately, that concept of government assistance is not accurate. The many disappointed and frustrated families are proof of that fact.

There *are* many good agencies and services available. If you have been disappointed in your contacts, remember that many agencies are understaffed and often poorly regulated. You may feel the workers you contact are apathetic and, of course, the paper work required of you seems endless.

Don't give up in despair! Stay calm no matter how frustrated you feel and try at all times to deal with these agencies and professionals in a courteous, pleasant and businesslike manner. I realize these people are public servants and they have no right to be indifferent to the needs of the public. It does help, however, to recognize that, while the professionals are sympathetic, they are very busy people. They simply do not have time to listen to a rambling account of each one of our problems. We, therefore, need to get to the point of our specific requests. Nothing disarms a frustrated social worker as readily as a kind, composed inquirer with a good sense of humor. Try it—you might be surprised! A very wise man once said, "A gentle answer turns away wrath, but a harsh word stirs up anger."[4]

Notes

1. Barbara Silverstone and Helen Kandel Hyman, *You and Your Aging Parent,* (New York: Pantheon Books, 1982), adapted from p. 150.
2. Jo Horne, *Care-Giving: Helping an Aged Loved One* (Glenview, IL: Scott, Foresman and Co., 1985), adapted from pp. 133-135.
3. Shirley Peterson, "Kitchen Hints Help Elderly with Their Chores," *The Ventura County Star-Free Press* (January 25, 1989), adapted from p. B-5.
4. Proverbs 15:1.

Chapter Six
The Caregiver

The week had been unusually hectic. The tasks of dashing to the hospital to visit my mother, doing her personal laundry, fulfilling my duties to my employer, meeting deadlines, giving adequate attention to my duties at church, plus numerous other responsibilities were almost more than I could endure. I felt pulled in dozens of directions. Inwardly, I knew that the real problem was not my workload, heavy as that was. My problem was that we would be celebrating Easter at the end of that week.

Holidays were always rough for me during the time my mother was confined to a convalescent hospital. Before her hospital days, Mom loved holidays because these days meant getting together with her children and grandchildren. She never complained when she was deprived of that joy while in the hospital, but my heart ached for her because I knew she missed the family festivities and being at home.

Despite my heavy schedule I went to the Good Friday service, taking my feelings of frustration, discouragement and depression with me. As the minister read the familiar account of the Crucifixion, several of the words suddenly took on new meaning for me. Although I had read the account many times, it had never occurred to me that the Son of God was deeply concerned about the welfare of *His* mother. Notwithstanding the great personal agony He suffered, He thought of Mary, His mother, standing at the foot of the cross. The Lord Jesus Christ made certain that she would be cared for. Speaking to His mother and to John, "the disciple whom he loved," Jesus said, "'Dear woman, here is your son,' and to the disciple, 'Here is your mother.'"[1] The Scripture tells us that from that time on John took Mary into his home, and we can be certain he cared for her.

Seated in that Good Friday service, I realized that my role as a caregiver had not changed. Somehow, though, knowing that the Lord's heart must have ached for His mother in her circumstance made the ache in my heart for my mother a bit lighter. I needed to be reminded that He understands all of our heartaches—even the exhausting task and the emotional strain of caregiving. I needed to remember that God always provides the needed strength as He did for me in that service, and to claim His continued provision for the future as I cared for my mother.

Caregiver Defined

In the foregoing chapters we considered ways and means of helping our parents who are still essentially living independent lives. These resources will, of course, continue to be of great help even as our parents become more dependent. Sadly, as age takes it toll on our parents and as they often become progressively more dependent, the big question facing a family is, who will become the main caregiver after parents become totally dependent?

At the time of this writing, the term "caregiver" does not appear in the *Merriam Webster's Ninth Collegiate Dictionary*. To avoid confusion, therefore, a clear definition is needed.

For a time social workers and experts in the field of gerontology used the word "caretaker," but some-

---

A caregiver is anyone who takes on the responsibility for the care of another person. Caregivers are important people and they come in all shapes and sizes.

---

time in the early 1980s a new term—"caregiver"—surfaced and it has become so widely used that it has replaced the original term. With so many people involved in the task of caring for the elderly and disabled, no doubt the term "caregiver" will soon make its official appearance in Webster.

A caregiver is anyone who takes on the responsibility for the care of another person. Caregivers are important people and they come in all shapes and sizes. There are no specific educational nor socio-economic requirements. Most caregivers find themselves in the role because a loved one is in need of care. One expert defined caregiver as "a euphemism for an unpaid female relative."

Who Are the Caregivers?

A caregiver may be a spouse, an adult daughter or son, a relative, a friend, a neighbor—you or me. Families, like individuals, are unique; therefore, there is a great variety in the way each family chooses the caregiver. Professionals in the field of family relations generally agree that, no matter how many adult children are in a family, the responsibility of caring for dependent parents usually falls to the women. It may be the oldest daughter who has children of her own, the youngest daughter who may still live at home with her parents, or even a daughter-in-law.

In 1985 the Travelers Corporation did an extensive survey of caregivers in the work place. They reported that nearly seven of every ten primary caregivers are women who spend an average of 16 hours a week in giving care. Men who are the primary caregivers average only five hour a week. The experts of this survey say that the reason for the difference in time devoted to care could be that the male's caregiving tends to take on such socially accepted male responsibilities as making home repairs or managing finances, rather than the physical nurturing care.[2]

Perhaps these findings are surprising in view of the changing role of women in our day. There was a time when the woman's role was limited to one pattern. She grew up, got married, raised her family and, finally, became the traditional grandmother, without the care of her own parents who had already died. Since World War II that role has been changing rapidly as more options opened to women. Add to that scenario the advancement in nutrition and medical science, which has extended the life expectancy of our generation, and you will find a vast number of women who become caregivers either by choice or of necessity.

The need for caregivers is tremendous. A study at Princeton University revealed that in the United States 65 percent of fifty-year-old women had living mothers in 1980, compared to only 37 percent with living mothers in 1940. The National Center for Health Service did a study on caregivers and reported that the average age of the persons surveyed was fifty-seven. One-third of those caregivers were *over* sixty-five years old. The study also indicated that only one-fourth of the caregivers surveyed rated their own health as fair or poor, as opposed to the three-fourths in good health. Financially, one-third of these persons were considered poor or near poor.[3]

In view of the fact that Medicare will not pay for the long-term care of an invalid and the fees for long-term care facilities are prohibitive to the average family funds, there is little choice. The only remaining alternative is for someone in the family to become a caregiver of a loved one.

The Spouse Caregiver

Persons who may automatically be drawn into the role of caregiver are wives who provide long hours of care in their own homes for their husbands. These are the women who are up in years. Their average age is between fifty-seven and sixty-five. At least 30 percent of them are older than seventy-four—women who often have health problems of their own. The hours these caregivers put in is amazing! Most give devoted care day and night, and that over and above their normal household duties. Many tend to give up their own personal social lives to become nursemaids to their lifetime companions. Others do so because they are totally unaware of services and benefits available to them to make their caregiving tasks a little easier. Families, therefore, need to be alert to a parent who is doing far more than he or she is able. Whether the parent will accept outside help or not, at least the overburdened caregiver should be aware of the available assistance.

When my father was diagnosed as having cancer, my mother was in her early sixties. For years she'd had heart trouble but had learned to live with it. Despite her age Mom was still working part-time outside their home when Dad became ill. There was, however, no thought in Mom's mind of having anyone else care for Dad.

During the five years that Dad struggled with cancer, Mom insisted she wanted to keep him at home as long as possible. Then one day in May my seventy-five-year-old father was rushed to the hospital very early in the morning. He died that same evening. Mom's prayers for strength and endurance to care for him had been answered. God had given her the ability to accomplish the task she felt so strongly she wanted to do.

I was living in the Chicago area at the time. When I arrived in California for the funeral, some of Mom's first words were, "I'm so glad I could care for him until the end." To Mom it was not only the loving thing a wife did; there was also a deep satisfaction and peace that she could care for her beloved. During the five years of Dad's illness, she relinquished that care only during the weeks he was in an acute care hospital.

No two accounts of caregiving are identical. Not all women are ready or even able to care for their ailing husbands. Some people find it extremely difficult to visit the sick in a hospital, let alone care for the sick—even a loved one. Others are not squeamish around people who are ill but they insist they are not the "nurturing type" and dislike caring for another. Despite their feelings they are often forced to become primary caregivers. Some who are financially able will hire assistant caregivers and have them either as live-ins or as visiting caregivers. When that fails, the disabled elderly is placed in an extended care facility.

The Only Child Caregiver

Caregiving should be shared by all of the adult children in a family. If, however, you are an only child, you would be wise to make every effort to stay in close contact with your aunts and uncles—your parents' siblings.

Although I am not an only child, my mother's youngest sister, my Aunt Alma, was like the Rock of Gibraltar for me during Mom's illness. Aunt Alma, my favorite aunt, was a registered nurse and, for years, had been my very dear friend. She lived in Colorado, and Mom and I were in California, but words can never describe what her counsel through letters, phone calls and visits meant to me. I knew I could call her anytime of the day or night and she would be there for me. She was a tremendous help and encouragement to us all.

If you have not done so in the past, begin now to build friendships by including your parents' siblings in some of your activities. Whether you have a long-standing friendship with your relatives or are working on a new one, it will be easier to call on them when the need arises. An aunt or uncle can be a great help in relieving your heavy caregiving load by providing transportation to and from the doctor's office, by parent-sitting when you are swamped or worn out, or just providing physical and emotional encouragement when you need it most.

It is easy for an only child to fall into the trap of placing unreasonable demands on him- or herself by insisting on carrying the entire responsibility of caregiving alone. It is next to impossible to carry that load single-handedly, so accept any help that friends or relatives offer to give. If you—because of pride, independence or whatever—continue to reject offered assistance, friends and relatives will soon back off. That means you have just closed a door on help you might need desperately now or in the near future. Furthermore, by continually rejecting offered assistance from your aunts or uncles, you may be responsible for deep, hurt feelings of rejection. Frequently, when an only child insists upon assuming all responsibility for caregiving, relatives experience feelings of being "shut out" of the lives of a beloved brother or sister.

If you are unfortunate and have no relatives living nearby, you will have to depend on some of the help already mentioned in earlier chapters, as well as suggestions found in chapter 7.

The Single Parent Caregiver

The superwoman of the '80s who is holding down a full-time job outside of the home often has all of the domestic responsibilities of managing a home, raising a family and attending school functions of her children, not to mention her church and community activities. In addition to that hectic schedule, many also have the responsibility of caring for a disabled parent. And countless women carry that load alone because, for any number of reasons, they are single parents—as in the case of Kim.

Kim's husband walked out on her, leaving her with their three children. She is a schoolteacher, but has only a B.A. degree. Finances are tight and frequently the children's father is late in sending his check for child support, at times even missing a payment entirely. Kim's school principal encouraged her to begin a study program in order to get her master's degree and thereby raise her salary level.

Kim made plans to enroll in summer school. Her ex-husband agreed to keep the children while she was in school. After summer school Kim planned to continue working on her degree by taking night school classes and perhaps manage another summer session the following year.

The work load was heavy, but the future appeared to be brighter for Kim. Two weeks into summer school, however, her parents were in an auto accident and Kim's mother was killed. Her father was rushed to a hospital.

Typical of summer school, Kim's study program was intense, demanding every moment of her time. The tragic accident changed her plans completely. She felt there was only one thing to do. Her father needed her so she dropped out of school, promising herself she would take the needed work later.

Kim's father recovered from his injuries but he seemed to have lost all reason to live without his spouse. His health deteriorated rapidly and he demanded more of Kim's time. She found herself in the "sandwich generation"—sandwiched between the demanding role of caring for her father on the one hand, and on the other, her responsibilities to her children, her job and her dire financial need, which required her to earn an advanced degree.

Being squeezed into that position can easily spell burnout. While mothering or nurturing loved ones is often a part of many women's instincts, the demands of the sandwich generation frequently leave the caregiver with feelings of anger, frustration, indignation and failure. The work load of adequately caring for family, an aging parent and a job becomes overwhelming. In their book *Aging Parents and You*, authors Anderson-Ellis and Dryan said of the sandwich generation, "It often means having to choose between two worlds, putting drops in our parents' eyes or wiping the tears from the eyes of our children."[4]

The Daughter Caregiver

Research shows that 80 percent of caregivers are the female adult children. Even when aging parents have an only son, the caregiver is usually the daughter-in-law.[5] From the beginning of time women have been associated with a nurturing role because they have always provided care when it was needed.

What about the son as a caregiver? According to the study cited earlier by the Travelers Corporation, only 29 percent of men provide primary care, and many of those men depend on their wives or outside help.

From my research for this book I discovered that the role for men and caregiving is changing. Many experts feel that, with shared roles of today's younger parents and the fact that younger fathers are assuming more of the child rearing duties, these men are acquiring more nurturing/caregiving skills. Eventually, the men will be more apt to step in when their parents need help.

The single parent is by no means the only caregiver who is caught in the sandwich generation. Countless caregivers are in it. One factor contributing to this is the career woman. She has spent a number of years developing a career and has, therefore, postponed having children until later. Postponement of parenthood plus the extended life expectancy of the aged means that the adult children today will, for the first time in American history, spend more time caring for their parents than caring for their children.

At the beginning of the century, parents could expect to provide for their children for about nineteen years, and only about nine years for their parents. Today, thanks to medical science, nutrition and increased life-span, it is estimated that parents will spend approximately seventeen years caring for their children and eighteen years caring for their own parents.[6] Small wonder that someone described middle-age as "the fifteen minutes between the time that our children go to college and we start to care for our aged parents."

Pitfalls to Avoid

Caregiving can be physically and emotionally exhausting; therefore, we need to be aware of the dangerous pitfalls that caregivers sometimes fall into.

Pitfall number one: Isolation. Many caregivers become so busy and tired out they find it is impossible to keep up their own social contacts outside their immediate family. Often they feel they cannot enjoy social activities even with the immediate family because "if we go out as a family, who will stay with Mother?" The loneliness that results from such demanding isolation can be devastating to the caregiver.

Being isolated from friends and deprived of other interests can also cause the caregiver to feel angry and resentful. There is a feeling of being betrayed, of feeling that other family members or friends have somehow let them down because they fail to offer assistance. Anger that is permitted to simmer inside without ventilation can often erupt with damaging effects. An angry, pressured caregiver who buries his feelings may be surprised when that anger suddenly explodes. When it does, the anger is often vented on the disabled person. No matter how loving the caregiver's original motives, when the caregiver is so isolated and overworked that anger goes out of control and is turned on the helpless, that caregiver becomes guilty of abuse. Abuse of the elderly will be discussed in more detail in chapter 9.

Pitfall number two: An unrealistic concept of caregiving. In view of the above tension and the emotional problems that can develop for the caregiver, we need to take a realistic look at several questions: Could it be that part of the pressure and tension is something the caregiver has brought on him- or herself? Is full advantage being taken of available services and help? Is there a realistic concept of the role of a caregiver? The caregiver needs to realize that caring for an older person is different from caring for a child. Caring for a disabled child, for example, is far more rewarding. Why? Because the prognosis for the child's improvement is usually quite good, especially for the child who is under the care of specialists. The child is often able to learn to function quite normally despite his handicap. Not so with the elderly person who is nearing the proverbial "threescore years and ten." The senior will *not* improve, but will worsen. That truth becomes depressing. As a result a caregiver tends to become very vulnerable and feels like a failure. That is why it is so important that the caregiver have outside interests, as well as support from other family members.

Pitfall number three: Hasty decisions. When death or a crisis arises in a family, adult children tend to feel that the best way to provide necessary comfort for the remaining parent is to bring that parent into the home of the adult child. Before you actually invite your parent to move into your home with you, think through that move and pray about it. "Oh," you say, "but my parents expect me to take them in and care for them." Are you sure that is what they really want?

Numerous studies have shown that, when given a choice, the older people prefer to remain in their own living quarters. They want to remain independent if at all possible because they do not want to become a burden to their children. While it may appear that taking your parent into your home is the best solution, it often presents problems for your spouse, your children, and for you—as well as your parent.

Most family counselors feel that there are not many elderly parents who can live peaceably with their grown children. The problems become even more pronounced, according to the experts, when it is a mother and daughter who are once again sharing living quarters, unless they have done so without friction for at least ten years. To move a mother into her daughter's home, and thereby threaten the elderly person's independence, often gives rise to mother-daughter conflicts that have been dormant for years. Old tensions between fathers and sons and even among siblings have also created problems. Obviously, a live-in arrangement too frequently presents far more problems than it solves.

Counselors say that a far better arrangement, if a move is unavoidable, is to find an apartment in the adult child's neighborhood or even in the same building, but where each party maintains privacy and independence.

An important fact to keep in mind is that studies show that parents do not want their children to care *for* them but to care *about* them. While they don't want to live *with* their children and become a burden, they want to be close enough so they can enjoy them and their grandchildren, and feel loved and not forgotten. Of course, parents appreciate children who help make arrangments for care when it is needed, but they do not want their children to provide that care.

Dr. Judith Alexandre, family counselor, stresses the importance of including the elderly parent in all family planning sessions when there is a need for additional care or a need for a change in living arrangements. For adult children to meet, make decisions and then announce the results to a parent who is still capable of understanding and thinking rather clearly smacks of a take-over. That action becomes very frightening to the elderly. To be told what is to be done without their input causes the elderly to doubt their own mental abilities and only adds to their list of fears.

Sibling adult children and the elderly parent should discuss the situation of needed care openly, honestly and kindly. Parents should have a say about all changes, whether it involves a live-in companion, moving into an apartment closer to the children, or a decision as small as beginning to have Meals on Wheels bring in one hot meal a day for the elderly.

Ready to Give Up?

Pressures and frustrations presented in this chapter leave little doubt that it is easy for a person to become

If you are a caregiver who feels you have reached the end of your rope,....by admitting your limitations you are not admitting failure....

so deeply involved with all the demands of caring for a disabled parent that a caregiver's physical and emotional health becomes endangered. The complaint I've heard expressed by numerous caregivers is the familiar, "I'm so tired! Everyone wants part of my time. I've had it!" Others feel that to admit they need help somehow spells failure. They feel they must keep going no matter what. Still other caregivers go on doing the impossible and then play the role of a martyr, complaining constantly but doing nothing to find help.

We have mentioned some of the exhausting duties of a caregiver, but we need to point out also that there often comes a time when it is okay to say, "I can't do anymore." If you are a caregiver who feels you have reached the end of your rope, may I be quick to assure you that by admitting your limitations you are not admitting failure. Rather, you are being sensible to recognize your need for assistance. If your health breaks down and you need care for yourself, your problems have only increased. No doubt your next question is: When does a caregiver know it's time to scream "H-E-L-P!"?

Modern Maturity magazine lists a number of danger signals that indicate the caregiver could use some help. Read the following complaints carefully:

- "No matter what I do, I just can't do enough for Mother. I don't have one minute for myself anymore."
- "My husband and children are being neglected. I just do not have time for them."
- "Instead of helping Mom and Dad now and then, these days I seem to be with them most of the time, either on the phone or at their house."
- "I know I shouldn't, but I feel so frustrated and angry! I'm stuck with all of this and no one offers to help anymore! Maybe I've rejected them too many times before."
- "I can't remember the last time our family—Jim, the kids and I—had time to laugh and play together."
- "This is a no-win situation! I feel *so* lonely!"[7]

Any of the above sound familiar? Are any of the statements an echo of your feelings? If so, chances are you are a candidate for burnout and in real need of help. The entire next chapter is given to suggesting available assistance and sources that the overworked caregiver may turn to for relief.

Notes

1. John 19:26-27.
2. John Wood, "Labors of Love" cited in *Modern Maturity* magazine, August-September 1987. Adapted.
3. Ibid, adapted.
4. Eugenia Anderson-Ellis and Marsha Dryan, *Aging Parents & You* (NY: Master Media Limited, 1988), p. 10.
5. Ibid.
6. Ibid.
7. Adapted from "Danger Signals that Say...Warning: Caregiver Needs Help!" *Modern Maturity* magazine, August-September 1987.

Chapter Seven
An SOS from Caregivers

Margaret felt worn out and discouraged. She and her seventy-eight-year-old husband, Lester, lived on a tight budget. Their Social Security checks plus Lester's small pension didn't allow for many extra luxuries. They had managed all right until Lester became ill, but for the past four years he had been suffering from Parkinson's disease and he was getting worse.

Margaret worried about their future. Until now she had been able to care for Lester, but she wondered how much longer she could handle the load. His care was becoming more demanding each day. Not only was she busy and tired all the time, but she was very lonely. These days Lester seemed to be in a world of his own. He seldom talked, was withdrawn and, at times, appeared bewildered. Margaret missed the closeness they used to enjoy. If only she could talk to someone! She couldn't leave Lester alone anymore, even to run an errand—and certainly not for an hour to go to church. Her deepest concern was one she hadn't really admitted to herself—she feared Lester had developed other complications.

Their son, Ron, lived nearby, but he was always so

busy that Margaret didn't want to bother him. Once, when she had hinted that his father was getting worse, she felt Ron had brushed her off. All he said was, "Mother, maybe you should get someone in to help you."

To Margaret, help meant extra expenses, and she wasn't sure they could afford it. What if the money wouldn't stretch far enough to take care of both of them? She and Lester always vowed never to be a burden to Ron. And now, after so many extra medical expenses not covered by Medicare, Margaret felt embarrassed about their lack of finances.

One day Beth, Margaret's daughter-in-law, stopped by just at the time when everything that could go wrong, did. Beth was quick to recognize Margaret's overload. Again she encouraged Margaret to contact the local Senior Citizen Association to find out whether there might be help available. Margaret was hesitant. She argued with Beth because of her fear of the unknown, as well as her concern for expenses. Within a few days, however, Ron and Beth persuaded her that she needed help. Ron immediately made contact with the local Community Mental Health Center. A friend stayed with Lester while Margaret and Beth went to find out what assistance was available—even for someone on a tight budget.

Much to Margaret's relief she found that a social worker was willing to come to their home to assess their needs and to discuss finances. Furthermore, she discovered her problems were not unique. She was assured it was not a sign of failure to admit she needed help and that her discouragement, loneliness and worries were very normal. The best news for Margaret was that she felt she was not alone. Help was available. "I didn't know they do all that!" she beamed, as she discovered some of the options available.

The SOS Signal

Whether you, like Margaret, are an older spouse with a "tired body" or a younger "sandwich generation" caregiver, you need to realize that the stress of the caregiver's role can lead to burnout. You need to know and then to admit to yourself that it's okay to send an SOS that says, "I can't take this anymore!" or "HELP!" Because caregiving is such an exhausting role, you frequently need a break.

In view of the fact that one-third of all caregivers are over the age of sixty-five, it means that most persons in that category are caring for a spouse, a parent or, frequently, both parents. Because these caregivers are themselves victims of the deterioration of age, the physical stress is gigantic. The elderly caregiver often neglects her own health and loses a lot of sleep. All night she is listening for noises from her care receiver or mate instead of sleeping. Neglecting her own personal needs, the elderly caregiver becomes a prime candidate for burnout or a physical breakdown. When that happens, everyone involved—the care receiver, the caregiver and, often, the entire family—suffers. That is why it is extremely important to be aware of what is happening if one of our parents is caring for the other. We must keep the lines of communication open so that our parents understand we are available to help out as needed.

Caregivers often have many reasons or excuses —some petty, others very real—for not getting help. An intense need for privacy is one reason. These caregivers feel they can handle the task on their own without "airing our problems" with outside help. Often this is the case when the care receiver has become incontinent and/or is sometimes mentally confused. Although very sincere, this excuse is not unlike the over-zealous housewife of our mothers' day who cleaned the house *before* the cleaning lady came in!

Other caregivers hesitate to seek assistance because they feel uncomfortable about having a stranger come into their homes. For some, the reluctance is due to an overwhelming feeling of guilt—guilt because to them it is an admission of wanting to get away from caregiving. People plagued by this guilt are far more concerned about what the neighbors will think than about their personal needs or the needs of their spouse and children. Closely related to the guilt feeling is the fact that the caregiver sincerely believes that no one is able to care for the parent as well as a family member—and usually that caregiver has reference to herself. Finally, some fail to seek assistance because they just do not know what help is available or how to go about finding that help.

Where to Find Needed Assistance

Community services are available, but finding the ones to meet your need can sometimes be frustrating and very time consuming. It is therefore important to become aware of what services are available while your parents are still maintaining a fairly independent life-style. When a crisis occurs and you are emotionally upset, needing help immediately, the stress of finding assistance can become overwhelming.

Usually we think of community resources first;

that is a good place to begin. But even then it is easier to find the appropriate agencies when you know what is available. Here is a list of just a few.

Government Agencies

At the top of the list is the Administration on Aging, Department of Health and Human Service, 200 Independence Avenue, S.W., Washington, D.C. 20201. This organization covers all areas of the needs of the elderly. Local branch offices on aging are located throughout the nation, but they may be listed under different names in your telephone directory. By calling your city hall, you should be able to get the name and phone number of the agency in your area that handles "Senior Information and Referral."

Local Department of Public Health

This department is often helpful, not only in suggesting assistance but also putting you in touch with the organizations in your community who have the services you need for your loved ones. In some cities the Department of Health publishes an excellent, helpful guide each year entitled "Resources Guide for Services for Seniors." When contacting the Health Department do not fail to ask about any published material they have available.

Local Churches

Check with local churches or synagogues to find out what helps, if any, they may have available. Some offer support groups for adult children, caregivers and families. One helpful program a number of churches sponsor was founded by gerontologist, Dr.

Richard P. Johnson. The program is called Caregivers of Older People (Co-OP).

National Health-related Organizations

Local branches of such organizations as the American Heart Association, the American Cancer Society, Alzheimer's Diseases and Related Disorders Association, the American Diabetes Association and numerous others offer help and guidance for persons afflicted with specific ailments. These organizations not only provide helpful information on certain diseases, they often direct families to available support groups in your area.

Local medical or gerontology departments may also provide guidance to help you meet your needs. Both departments should be able to verify or veto any listings you may find in your telephone directory in the White Pages as well as the public services listed in the Yellow Pages under "Home Health Services." Needless to say, it is well to discuss any organizations or agencies listed in the phone book with a professional before placing a loved one in the care of people or an organization you know little about.

While seeking available help, don't overlook the assistance you may find from your own family doctor, or your parents' physician, nurses or social workers.

How to Reach Government Agencies

To suggest to a busy caregiver that he or she contact a government office usually results in a set-jaw look and a "You-no-doubt-have-never-tried-to-get-through" response. May I assure you that I have! May I also ask you to please not cross off all city, county or state offices from your list immediately!

For years I hated to call these agencies. I felt frustrated because usually their lines were busy or I was put on hold or shuffled from one person to the next. Of course, with each new person to whom my call was given, I had to start all over from the beginning with my request. The most maddening truth was that, despite all my efforts, I was still often unsuccessful in getting an answer to my question! I'm sure that sounds familiar and you can readily identify. I soon realized most of these agencies are under-staffed, but that didn't solve my problem.

The amazing truth is that this run-around is not limited to government agencies for the elderly. While writing this chapter, I had to take time out for some tests at a medical clinic. About mid-morning the R.N. who was administering my tests received a phone call from her very frantic housekeeper. It took a few moments before the nurse could ascertain that a water pipe in her home had apparently broken. The housekeeper insisted that water was "gushing out of the wall," but she didn't know how to turn off the water.

The nurse immediately called the water department. Despite explaining to each person she reached that she could *hear* the water "gushing" as she talked to her housekeeper, each one suggested another phone number the nurse should call.

You guessed it—with each new number she had to retell her story, as visions of damaged plaster, soaked rugs and warped floors danced through her head. By actual count the nurse called *six* different phone numbers before she found someone who could shut off that water!

An SOS from Caregivers

In a book entitled *Caring for Your Parents*, author Helene MacLean provides some hints that I am sure you will find helpful. Clearly she writes from experience as she promises such frustration as being given a run-around, busy signals, being disconnected—and all that while being on hold! In fact, her comments are so realistic she could have been listening in on a few of my attempts to reach local or state agencies. MacLean, however, encourages people to "be patient and persistent" despite these frustrations. Don't give up. You can get answers as well as help.

In view of the frustrations callers frequently experience, Helene MacLean suggests first that, when consulting an agency, you must allow plenty of time. If you don't expect your phone call to produce answers to your questions within five minutes, you won't become upset. If, however, you are pressed for time, chances are you will become irritated by the delays or by being shuffled from one person to another. When you become upset, your irritability and frustration become contagious.

Next, prepare for the call *before* you even dial the number. Have a notebook in hand (preferably a loose-leaf to allow for expansion). Reserve one page for each call. Write down the date of your call, the name of the agency, their phone number and the specific questions you want to ask. Leave enough space after each question so that you might *briefly* jot down notes on the answers you receive.

When someone answers your call, ask for the person's name to whom you are speaking and write it down. This is most helpful for any future calls. With that information in hand, you are now ready to ask your questions and to make brief notes on the answers. If the person to whom you are speaking is unable to help you, try to find out what agency to call, the phone number if possible and the name of the person for whom to ask. The more basic information you can gather, the better.

Suppose, instead of a phone call, you are paying a personal visit to an agency. MacLean deals with that also, and again says preparation is a must. Bring your prepared notebook, as well as something to do while you wait—a book to read, needlepoint, stationery or whatever.

When entering an office and before you settle down to wait for the person you have come to see, talk to the receptionist and clearly state the purpose of your call. Believe me, you will save time by making sure you are in the correct office and haven't been directed to the wrong place. If you discover there has been an error in the directions you received, find out where you need to go, as well as the name of the person who can help you. Be sure to write down the names given to you.[1]

Just as you did on the phone calls, why not take your notebook with you so that you may jot down the information you receive, as well as names to whom you may need to refer in the future? Or, take a pocket-size tape recorder and a microcassette tape with you. You will, of course, need to ask permission to record the interview before you do so. Both the notebook and the tapes will be most helpful if it becomes necessary to check back or verify information you received.

No doubt you will find most government employees helpful and understanding. Should you run into incompetency or even rudeness from some of the lower-level employees, it is helpful to write down their names so that you may speak to their supervisors at a later date. Government employees are public servants and you do not need to put up with inconsiderate behavior. On the other hand, when you receive help from a department over a longer period of time, you might send a note of appreciation to them or to their superiors. Appreciation for a job well done accomplishes far more than complaints.

Coping and Caregiving

Recently one of my nieces, a young mother of two small children, indicated that some of the most difficult times in infant care are the first few months. Every waking moment seems to be given to that baby, and night feedings are very much a part of the round-the-clock care. "Losing so much sleep during those first weeks is almost the worst part of having a baby!" she insists.

Young mothers are often physically drained due to lack of sleep and recovering from the stress of pregnancy. The good news is that eventually the baby will sleep through the night and the worn out mother can catch up on her own sleep. Not so with the person faced with the responsibility of caring for an elderly disabled person. The care demanded resembles a 36-hour rather than a 24-hour-day, and interrupted sleep can continue for years, as demonstrated by a caregiver I interviewed recently.

Phoebe had no brothers or sisters and she was looking forward to her own retirement. Her plans were made—she would travel and do many of the things she'd not had time for before.

Then her mother was diagnosed as having a dementing illness. Patients who suffer from this illness have difficulty remembering; often their ability to reason, understand or use good judgment is impaired. Phoebe's father was up in years and in very poor health.

Instead of seeing her own plans for retirement develop, Phoebe found herself deprived of all personal time as her mother's condition worsened rapidly. Because of the nature of her mother's illness, Phoebe had little choice but to place her into a nursing home while she cared for her father. Eventually he, too, became so feeble he had to be moved into his daughter's home.

As she spoke of the strenuous schedule of caring for her disabled parents, Phoebe's comment was, "I think my greatest fear was that I might not be strong enough to handle the emotional heartbreak involved, and still continue the myriad duties demanded of me!"

When her father continued to decline, Phoebe found help from Hospice Care in her local city. Phoebe could not praise Hospice enough for the wonderful help she received, which included visitation in the home from a registered nurse three times a week, plus the services of a nurse's aide several times a week. With tears trickling down her cheeks, Phoebe told me about the compassion and concern Hospice Care extended to her when her father died. "They took care of everything!" she said.

Hospice Care

Many families are not acquainted with this program because they have not had a need for its services. The first Hospice originated in London, England, led by a British physician, Dame Cicely Saunders. She called her program the Saint Christopher's Hospice. Due both to her deep concern for the suffering as well as her caring for the terminally ill, Dame Cicely Saunders expanded her own professional skills of nursing to become a social worker and, eventually, a physician. In speaking of the establishment of hospice she said, "I couldn't have done it without my spiritual foundations."

The hospice movement in our country received its inspiration and guidance from Saint Christopher's Hospice. The first hospice program in the United States started in 1974 at Yale University in New Haven, Connecticut.[2] Presently, there are at least 1,715 hospice programs scattered across the United States, many of which are accredited for Medicaid payment.

Hospice care is for patients who are terminally ill—those whose doctor has verified that life expectancy has deteriorated to a matter of time. This care is offered to help patients and their families cope with death and dying. When possible, care takes place in the patient's home rather than in a hospital, but it is around-the-clock care. The patient has the choice to die at home. The patient also has a choice concerning pain and is permitted to have family members —including pets—nearby. Visitors may come at any time the patient wishes to have them. In addition to caring for the patient, a hospice will also train family members and friends how to care for the patient in as many aspects of caregiving as the family can handle.

A former director of the National Hospice Organization, Ms. Louise Bracknell, once said that members of the organization "see the person as a social, spiritual and psychological being. We treat the patient and family as a unit." They do whatever they can to relieve the pain and make the patient's remaining time as comfortable and pain-free as possible. As in the case of my friend Phoebe, most hospice programs provide support for family members during times of bereavement. They do what they can to ease the pain, even to the extent of providing months of counseling for the grief-stricken family, if necessary, after the patient's death.

A list of local care centers is available from: The

The purpose of most support groups is to provide relief for the overworked caregiver. [They] help the caregiver learn more about giving care and...make the job a little easier.

National Hospice Organization, 1901 North Fort Myer Drive, Suite 401, Arlington, Virginia 22209, phone 703-243-5900. Often your local hospitals, Medicare, doctors, visiting nurses association and private insurance companies can direct you to a Hospice Care unit in your area.

Support Groups

In an attempt to provide practical, helpful and relevant information for readers of this book, I interviewed numerous adult children who are presently, or have been, caregivers. The comment I heard over and over again was that "being a caregiver is a very lonely job." Most expressed the same feeling I felt when caring for my mother: Surely my family and I are the *only* ones who are going through this traumatic time of heartache as the rest of the world rushes by! How I longed for someone to talk with who would understand the mixed emotions I was experiencing at the time—but I found no one.

Two caregivers whom I interviewed today both said, in effect, "We need each other. We can talk and compare. We can support one another and sometimes we can laugh together—or cry together." And that is the purpose of most support groups. Now, please don't throw your hands up in despair and, in no uncertain terms, insist, "I don't have time to do *one* extra thing, nor do I have one extra hour to attend some meeting! Frankly, why should I listen to others talk about their problems? I have enough of my own!"

Granted, you are busy. You have more than your share of demands on your time, but let me tell you about support groups. They are not just crying sessions—unless that is your primary need at that moment. If so, you will find understanding, compassionate supporters ready to help you. The purpose of most support groups is to provide relief for the overworked caregiver. Their meetings are sessions designed to help the caregiver learn more about giving care and, with the knowledge of more efficient ways to handle the patient, to make the job a little easier.

Support groups can provide vital information about helpful tips, aids and services available in your area and to give you, the caregiver, an opportunity to socialize with people who are sympathetic, understanding and able to identify with your problems without a lot of explanations on your part.

Usually there is a group leader who is either a gerontologist or a professional from the medical field. The leader makes arrangements for the meeting and either leads or schedules programs and discussions. Programs are closely geared to the needs of the participants. This means that those in attendance are encouraged to share experiences, not only to ventilate pent-up

Support groups will not make a caregiver's week any shorter, but the love and understanding of others...in a like situation helps to ...lift the overwhelming burden.

emotions, but to enable the leader or some other expert to respond to questions any group members may have. Answers usually include helpful techniques and suggestions that are beneficial to the entire group.

Caregivers who have participated in support groups are usually quick to admit that it takes a great deal of schedule juggling and a lot of effort to find time to attend. All agreed, however, the emotional benefits were well worth the effort. One caregiver summed up her feelings as she said, "I just couldn't have survived without the group. Thanks to them and the guidance I got there, I was able to recognize and to deal with my depressing guilt feelings." Another said, "I was so tied up in knots that I was surprised when I found myself laughing with our group—something I hadn't done for weeks—and that about something people outside of our group probably wouldn't think was funny!"

How do you find support groups in your area? Often, national health-related organizations such as the American Cancer Society or the National Alzheimer's Disease and Related Disorders Association have support groups, or they can direct you in finding groups in your area. Another resource is to write to National Support Center for Families of the Aging, P.O. Box 245, Swarthmore, Pennsylvania 19081 and/or Family Caregivers Program, National Council on Aging, 600 Maryland Avenue, S.W., Washington, D.C. 20024.

If, after making such contacts, you are still unsuccessful in locating a support group, why not appeal to that friend or relative who sometime in the past has offered to help "if you ever need it." Ask that person to start a support group in your neighborhood. The following list of procedures will help launch a group.

1. Think of other people in your church, neighborhood, place of work or among your friends who are now in the role of caring for an aged parent or friend.
2. Make a list of their names, addresses and phone numbers.
3. Contact each one to find out if they would be interested in meeting for an hour or two to discuss the problems and needs of the caregiver.
4. Contact a professional—a social worker, a nurse, a

gerontologist or counselor—and ask if that person would be willing to meet with a group of over-worked caregivers.

5. Find a place that is centrally located for the meeting. Perhaps the professional can make suggestions, or you might contact your church or the local library about a meeting place.

6. The first meeting should be an informal time of getting acquainted. Have name tags available for each one (a 3x5 card, a felt tip pen, and straight pins for each card is all you need). Suggest that the participants introduce themselves to the rest of the group, then briefly describe their caregiving situations.

7. Ask the professional to present the purpose and value of a local support group.

8. As interest for a support group becomes evident, let participants decide how often to meet. When? Where? How long? Ask for suggested program topics the people want to discuss. Experts in the field report that the most successful support groups are those in which the participants choose their own topics for discussion and direct their own programs.

9. Be sure to have interested participants sign a mailing list with correct addresses and phone numbers, in order to send notices of upcoming meetings.

10. In addition to a leader you may want to have the group appoint a secretary. Decide whether you need to have dues (only to defray expenses for mailing announcements or for refreshments, if the group so desires).

11. Ask for volunteers who will be willing to share

their experiences or helpful techniques they have discovered. This will be the program for the next meeting. You may want to plan programs for the next several meetings, based on the group's suggestions (see point 8).

12. Plan to spend most of the support group meeting time providing opportunities for members to share, to socialize and to gain new knowledge that will make their work a little easier. *Keep the business meetings short.* The purpose of the group is to support, comfort and help each participant.[3]

Support groups will not make a caregiver's week any shorter, but the love and understanding of others who are in a like situation can help to bring a measure of relief and lift the overwhelming burden. The Bible says, "God, the Father of our Lord Jesus Christ...gives us comfort in our trials so that we in turn may be able to give the same sort of strong sympathy to others in theirs."[4] That is what support groups under good leadership can do for the caregiver, because that is what support groups are all about.

Notes

1. Helene MacLean, *Caring for Your Parents a Guidebook of Options and Solutions for Both Generations,* (New York: Doubleday, 1987), adapted from pp. 3-5.
2. Florence Walk, "The Widening Scope of Spiritual Care," *The American Journal of Hospice Care,* Volume 6, Number 4, July/August 1989, adapted from pp. 40,41.
3. Jo Horne, *Caregiving-Helping an Aging Loved One,* an AARP Book, (Glenview, IL: Lifelong Learning Div., 1985), adapted from pp. 271-272.
4. 2 Corinthians 1:3-4, Phillips.

Chapter Eight
The Maze of Extended Care and Finances

If you have continued reading this far, you are aware that gerontologists insist elderly people should be permitted and encouraged to remain independent as long as possible. The longer they can maintain an independent life-style, the better off they are even if they need to draw on the assistance of available community resources. We cannot ignore the fact, however, that the U.S. Senate Special Committee on Aging reports that one in five older Americans eventually needs long-term care. Most of them receive the care at home, but currently 1.4 million Americans are in nursing homes because, in some cases, home care has become impossible. Ralph is a case in point.

Physical therapy and tender loving care from his wife, Janet, finally got Ralph out of bed and into a wheelchair after his first stroke. He improved greatly at home and eventually began walking again, despite his impaired right leg.

Five years later, Ralph fell and broke his hip. When he returned home after surgery and a lengthy hospital stay, Janet took on the extra care involved. She was in her early seventies and the extra duties began to aggravate some of her own chronic health problems.

Several months later when Janet's physical and emotional situations were close to a breaking point, Ralph had another stroke. Now he was confined to his bed at times, and the work load for Janet was even greater. The stroke left Ralph slightly confused and frequently he did not recognize Janet or know where he was.

The emotional strain was rough. Janet worried that on his many visits to the bathroom during the night Ralph would fall and lie helpless on the floor before she could summon help, or that in his mental confusion he would wander away from home. Ralph's condition now demanded all of Janet's time. For her it meant the loss of many hours of needed rest, and the heavy responsibilities continued to take a great toll on her health and well-being.

Janet's doctor encouraged her to put Ralph into a nursing home, but she could not bring herself to do so. She finally talked to their sons about Ralph's condition and the doctor's recommendation. Both men immediately voiced their objections. Unfortunately, one son lived in Iowa, the other in Florida. Neither offered to come to relieve their mother or help in any way.

The decision was up to Janet and it was heartrending. Not only was Ralph no longer the strong one who always took on the greater responsibility of difficult decisions, the aging process had robbed Janet of her best friend, as well. Sadly, she finally realized that the time had come to let go—although her realization didn't make it any easier. Through her tears she said,

"To think that after forty-six years of marriage I can't take care of him anymore!"

Money was not a particular problem and, with the help of their pastor and her physician, Janet found a fine nursing home for Ralph. Eventually she was able to admit in her heart what she already knew in her mind—she had made the right decision. She knew she

---

To release someone into an extended care facility does not mean the caregiver has failed. The caregiver role continues, but to a lesser degree.

---

had done the right thing. Her loved one could now receive the twenty-four-hour-a-day care he so desperately needed. And with that care, she could still spend time with him without endangering her own health with overload.

To release someone to an extended care facility is never easy. It takes great courage to admit that you, as a caregiver, have done all you can for your loved one. Now that loved one's condition is such that you need to let go before your own health is damaged. Or perhaps the need is your own family, who may have been neglected as a result of your heavy involvement in caregiving.

Because a caregiver tends to become so vulnerable, we again need to be reminded of an important truth: To release someone into an extended care facility *does not* mean the caregiver has failed. The caregiver role continues, but to a lesser degree, to be sure. Frequent visits offer reassurance that the elderly has not been abandoned. The role of the caregiver now is to provide that kind, loving support necessary to get through the initial period of adjustment, to make new friends, to become acquainted with a new routine and to participate in any activities the facility may provide.

Admitting a parent to an extended care facility does not necessarily mean this is a permanent arrangement. You may consider a short-term stay away from home for the elderly before making a decision on a nursing home. A short-term stay often prepares the care receiver as well as the caregiver for the time when long-term care becomes a necessity.

Adult Day Health Care Centers

An adult day care center may be the answer for a short-term stay for an elderly person who is trying to regain strength after a bout with the flu, or who is recovering from surgery and cannot stay alone at this stage. The problem is that not all areas have these centers available.

According to the National Council on Aging, the cost for adult day health care centers is usually about thirty dollars a day, depending on the services offered. That price may appear to be high, but when you consider that private nursing care runs from ten to thirty dollars *an hour*, and the average cost in a nursing home runs from fifty to ninety dollars a day (and often more), the day health care cost is most reasonable.

In a day care center the patient comes home at night and the family may choose how many days each week the elderly person will spend at the center.

The caregiver and the elderly (if able) need to consider several factors in selecting a day care center. Dorothy Howe, program coordinator for the National Institute on Adult Day Care, suggests the following guidelines:

1. Make sure the center is certified or licensed by your state.
2. Investigate the ratio of staff to patient. Howe suggests the ratio should not be more than eight patients to one staff member, and lower for programs where patients require extra attention. Not all centers hire registered or licensed nurses; some employ social workers only. In that case, you need to inquire if the social workers are trained to do CPR.
3. Ask how emergencies are handled. Will the staff contact the family immediately?
4. If the center provides food and your parent is on a special diet, is the center able to accommodate that need?
5. Talk to the activities director and find out what activities are being offered and how often they are available.
6. In addition to the daily fees, are there any extra fees, such as money for transportation, etc.? Is there any state or federal aid available? If so, what procedures are necessary to secure that aid should it be needed?[1]

The Nursing Home

To most people, regardless of age, the words "nursing home" have a frightening connotation. To many the term is synonymous with terms like neglect, loneliness, rejection, failure and cruelty. At best the words may mean stern, sterile, regimented care.

We have all heard the horror stories about some facilities, but we cannot make a blanket statement indicating that *all* nursing homes are bad. True, according to recent media coverage, there are far too few good ones, but they *are* available. Experts in the field of aging report that the majority of the nursing homes fall somewhere between the very poorly operated ones and the excellent homes.

To eliminate any confusion about the term that often creates such negative mental images, we will define "nursing home." It is a broad term that covers several different types of care facilities. We usually think of nursing homes as being for the elderly who have come to the end of the trail. In reality, the facility can be a home for all ages. Some are for patients who are recovering from an accident or serious illness; some are for patients of drug abuse; others are for all ages of mentally retarded persons. In some cases a nursing home can be a type of halfway home for temporary placement while arrangements are being made for other extended care. It can also serve as a temporary respite for an exhausted caregiver while the family is on vacation for a few days.

A nursing home is different from an acute care hospital in that it is not for patients who are gravely ill. It is a facility for people of all ages who have difficulty caring for themselves. For our purposes in this book, we will think of a nursing home as a facility for the elderly.

There are two different types of nursing homes—designated by the care offered in the facility:

1. *Skilled Nursing Facilities (SNF)*—This facility is for patients who require skilled nursing twenty-four hours a day and it is most like an acute care hospital. The length of a patient's stay depends on the prognosis of the physician. While many elderly remain permanently, some patients will be discharged when their doctors feel they are sufficiently rehabilitated after a serious illness like a major stroke or heart attack.

The SNF provides not only medical supervision but also rehabilitation as needed, and the staff monitor chronic or unstable conditions of patients.

Staff, as the name SNF implies, includes registered and licensed practical nurses—who take their orders from an attending physician—and nurses' aides. A convalescent hospital is one example of an SNF facility.

2. *Intermediate Care Facilities (ICF)*—Patients in this type of nursing home are often mobile and, normally, not all are confined to their beds. Regular nursing services are provided—but not on a twenty-four hour basis—with registered nurses on hand. Usually, at least one R.N. on a nursing shift per twenty-four hours is required.

The ICF staff is made up of registered and licensed practical nurses, a therapist or two, and nurses' aides. Many of the ICF facilities provide a limited program of therapy for patients who have suffered a stroke or injury. In most cases, care for the patients in an ICF facility is considered to be "custodial" care.

Some nursing homes offer both levels of care—skilled nursing and intermediate care. There is a distinct advantage for the patient in a facility that offers both levels of care. As the patient's condition improves or deteriorates, transfer to the level of care needed can be done with very little trauma. Such a transfer is certainly far easier than searching for a new facility and moving the patient each time a different level of care is required.

Nursing Home Ownership

In searching for a nursing home you need to be aware that there are basically three types of nursing home ownerships:

1. *Nonprofit homes* are run by religious, fraternal, union and community groups, many with private endowments. Because these homes are subsidized by their parent organizations (by religious or fraternal groups), care in these facilities is sometimes less expensive.

2. *Government/public nonprofit* are the institutions operated by government agencies—city, county, state—that provide various levels of care.

3. *For-profit facilities* are privately owned and, as the name implies, they are operated to earn the highest profit for owners. Nursing homes owned by private individuals or corporations are big business. Statistics indicate that currently there are more than 23,000 nursing homes with more than 1.5 million beds. Eighty percent of these nursing homes in the United States are reported to be privately owned, and the industry is growing. Approximately thirty-two companies operated 17 percent of all nursing homes in 1983. It is projected by corporate officials that the number will increase so that 50 percent of all beds will

be in homes owned and operated by five to ten companies by 1990.[2]

The argument for privately owned nursing homes is that they provide a much higher quality of care than the other two types; however, that is not always the case.

In many families there are two topics that adult children and their parents frequently fail to discuss: the subject of finances and death.

Bills! Bills!

It has been said that in many families there are two topics that adult children and their parents frequently fail to discuss: the subject of finances and the subject of death. (We will discuss death in chapter 11.) With the high cost of medical expenses in our day there is nothing that is more threatening or worrisome to the elderly than that they will run out of money and be unable to pay their bills, or that they will need to accept financial aid from their children. Tragically, cost will often be the deciding factor in selecting a nursing home for your parent. Perhaps you have already discovered that neither Medicare, Medicaid nor private insurance programs cover *all* bills.

147

To avoid some of the confusion that seems to be rampant among adult children as well as the elderly, let's look very briefly at the two government programs established under the Social Security Administration to help defray medical expenses. You need to contact your local offices for detailed information because space does not permit solving all the confusion surrounding the federal and state insurance programs.

Medicare

This federal health insurance program is administered by the Social Security Administration throughout the United States for persons sixty-five years old and older. It has two sections: Part A and Part B. The first section *helps* to pay for hospital care, *but does not pay all*. It covers some post-hospital care while a patient is recuperating in a skilled nursing facility for up to one hundred days ONLY when a physician indicates a patient's condition requires that service. Unfortunately, at the present time federal, state and most private insurance companies consider most extended care for the chronically ill to be custodial care, and neither federal nor state will pay.

Part B of Medicare *helps* to pay for the services of physicians, some medical supplies and some therapy. Under certain conditions Part B will pay for part-time skilled nursing care in a patient's private home. There are, however, many medical expenses that Medicare does not cover. Furthermore, many medical facilities and physicians will not accept the standard for fees established by Medicare. It is very important, therefore, to talk to your parent's physician to discover in advance what the doctor's policy is.

148

Similar to other insurance programs, Medicare participants must apply for membership, and there is a monthly fee for all Medicare members. This fee changes from time to time; thus, you or your parent need to call your local Social Security office to find out what the current fee is.

Be forewarned that there are many, many Medicare forms to fill out in order to receive payment. The Medicare offices all across the country indicate that a large percentage of the forms they receive for payment from the elderly and their families are incomplete or incorrectly filled out due to a lack of knowledge of what services Medicare covers.

Both you and your parents need to become acquainted with the policies and services of Medicare *before* you face a crisis. A pamphlet that I found most helpful is entitled "Your Medicare Handbook." It is available without cost at any Social Security office.

Medicaid

This insurance program, like Medicare, is part of the Social Security Act. Medicaid is different from Medicare in that it is funded by federal *and* state governments; therefore, the benefits will differ from state to state. The name may even vary in different states. In California, for example, this program is called Medi-Cal. It is administered by your local social service departments. To obtain benefits from Medicaid the participant must apply at a local social service office listed in the telephone directory under Department of Social Services or the Department of Welfare.

Like Medicare, Medicaid was also established to assist the needy with hospital and medical expenses. Basically, Medicaid covers such services as outpatient hospital services, home health services, and even some inpatient hospital services. In some states items like prescription drugs, dental services and eyeglasses are covered. Do not assume, however, that your state covers the items I have listed. You need to contact your local public health office or your social service office to discover what benefits are available from Medicaid in your state. In some areas an individual may be eligible for benefits from both Medicaid and Medicare at the same time.

Be aware that Medicaid assistance is available to those without major medical insurance, but only *after* private assets are almost depleted. At the time of writing this book California recipients need to "spend down" so that private assets are no more than $2,000. Although that amount is very small in this day of high-cost living, it is to be considered funds for funeral expenses for the recipient.

Supplemental Assistance

There is a federal program available for the elderly who are sixty-five and older, who are blind and/or disabled, and have inadequate resources. These persons may apply for additional income through a program called Supplemental Security Income (SSI).

To be eligible for benefits from SSI the recipient's income cannot exceed a certain amount, and assets are limited to a minimum. When checking assets Social Security officials will examine unearned income, such as pensions, interest, etc., plus earned income such as wages. The recipient may own a house and a car with a limited retail value, but anything else—savings and/or checking accounts, stock and bonds—will count as resources. The individual's resources cannot be more than $1,600, or $2,400 for a couple. This amount increases every year; therefore, it is important to verify the amount at your local Social Security office when considering application for SSI benefits.

The requirements for eligibility for SSI are standard all across the United States; however, the benefits vary in individual states. For example, in some states if a person qualifies for SSI, eligibility for Medicaid benefits is automatic, even without having to apply for those benefits. State supplements are subject to change; thus, it is unwise to assume anything pertaining to SSI benefits without first checking with your local Social Security office.

My research indicates that many older people do not take advantage of SSI benefits despite the fact that they qualify. Some feel these benefits are like welfare payments rather than Social Security supplements; pride prevents them from accepting what could rightfully be theirs. Others do not claim these benefits because they are unaware of the SSI program.

Private Medical Insurance

There are numerous supplementary health insurance policies available to help cover the gaps that Medicare and Medicaid fail to cover. Unfortunately, many major medical policies that cover catastrophic illness will not continue that coverage for the policyholder after age sixty-five—the age when that coverage is often needed most desperately.

Many policies for long-term care are becoming very popular, but they are known to be expensive. And some of these policies are not always what they appear to be. In an article in *Consumer Reports* a number of cases were cited where insurance companies sold long-term care policies to trusting individuals, but failed to pay the elderly policyholders when claims were submitted.

In reporting on a study, *Consumer Reports* said, "Our May 1988 report found many policies for long-term care to be expensive and riddled with loopholes. The picture has improved, but it is still far from perfect."[3]

In view of this statement and the recent unfavorable media reports concerning long-term care insurance, it would seem wise not to be too quick to sign on the dotted line of a long-term care policy. Of course, no one knows in advance what an insurance company will pay when claims are submitted, but you and your parent need to be aware that there are loopholes in many policies.

What, then, is the answer for mounting medical expenses for senior citizens? Increased health protection for the elderly! While some effort is being made by some of the larger action groups promoting welfare for the elderly, much more needs to be done.

Who Is in Charge?

What happens when your parent becomes incapacitated and is no longer able to assume responsibility for managing financial affairs? Who takes over? Who is in charge?

Authors Florence Shelley and Jane Otten, in their book *When Your Parents Grow Old*, indicate that most American families have no plan of action, including medical and financial arrangements, should an emergency or crisis arise.[4]

As we see the years slip by, all of us are aware that the day may come when incompetency strikes our loved one. We, however, dislike the thought. It is painful, and often there is still a bit of the shame and stigma buried deep in our hearts that, at one time, was associated with mental illness. That shame and stigma may rise to the surface when we become aware that our parents are beginning to show signs of mental deterioration. It is not uncommon to hear stories of people who failed to make financial arrangements until *after* a major illness or mental deterioration has left the elderly too impaired to assume the financial responsibility any longer.

In an attempt to avoid many legal hassles after a crisis, advanced planning is vitally important. While your parents are still able to do so, they should consult with an attorney for estate planning. Then, when illness or death comes, their wishes can be executed in the manner they desired. If they cannot afford an attorney there are programs available that provide both legal advice and representation in court for the elderly on low incomes.

Power of Attorney

The most difficult problem associated with advance planning is often the elderly person. Age has robbed them of so much of their independence that it is often difficult for an older person to give any financial power even to a son or a daughter. Tragically, some elderly have reasons for this reluctance because adult children have been known to rob parents who were thought to be too old to know they were being swindled.

Your parent should have a strong voice in choosing the person who is to handle finances when that need becomes a reality. You will need an attorney to help you prepare for the proper legal actions.

State laws vary, but it is possible to establish a *power of attorney* or a *durable power of attorney*. The power of attorney is a written, legal document in which your parent gives you, or another responsible person, the power and permission to manage his or her financial funds. When, however, your parent becomes incompetent that power ends, unless it has been stated in writing beforehand (while the parent was still of a sound mind) that the power is to continue even in the event that the parent becomes incapacitated.

A power of attorney can also be revoked at any time your parent (the principal) wishes to do so. Suppose your father died and your mother is too upset to handle the sale of some real estate they owned together. If your parents had each conferred this power on the other, your mother might appoint you as power of attorney to sell the real estate and to take care of the legal transactions involved.

The durable power of attorney is more sophisticated than the simple power of attorney in that the document continues after the elderly person becomes incompetent or incapacitated. Since 1982 those with the durable power of attorney in California not only have power over financial matters, but medical and health care decisions, as well.[5] The distinct advantage of this unique legal instrument is that it provides opportunity for the elderly person to give specific instructions ahead of time as to what medical treatments they want or do not want.

I shall be eternally grateful to my mother for clearly expressing to us—her children—that she absolutely did not want heroic measures and life-sustaining equipment when the time came for her to die. She was very competent when she informed us in no uncertain terms that she and the Lord were on good terms; she knew where she was going "when my time comes" and she did not want anyone to interfere "when the Lord calls me home!"

The durable power of attorney document can relieve the family of some very difficult decisions, should the need arise, enabling the family to carry out their parents' wishes for or against heroic and life-sustaining methods.

In many states the durable power of attorney is limited to financial powers only. Therefore, you need to have your attorney clearly define what is involved in this legal instrument in your state.

Guardianship

What happens if your loved one has a stroke and becomes incompetent *before* you have power of attorney of any kind? Again, state laws vary and if your loved one has become disabled to the point of no longer understanding or accounting for personal assets and property, you need to seek legal advice.

In some states the only legal procedure is often a painful one for the family because it means they must have their loved one declared incompetent by the courts. This incompetency procedure can sometimes become rather complicated, because to have a person declared incompetent usually involves a physician's certification concerning the patient's mental condition. After the incompetent declaration the local probate court will then appoint a guardian, who may or may not be a family member, to manage the financial affairs and/or the estate.

Finally, a very important issue between adult children and parents is honesty, love and an open spirit of decision making. Both parents and children should be involved in making decisions concerning matters to be handled. Discuss financial and estate planning as early as possible and, hopefully, before the parents become disabled. Get as much information as you can regarding the laws of your state involving your estate and other legal safeguards. Secure the best legal advice you can afford. Many communities offer guidelines at no cost.

Have you and your parents made a will? Do you understand what your parents want their will to accomplish, especially in the case of a living spouse? Has a power of attorney been appointed? What insurance policies do your parents have? Local bankers, the legal aid society or your Area Agency on Aging can offer many suggestions to make caregiving involving finances and legal matters easier, and will help you avoid surprises when crises arise.

Notes

1. Maggie Bendicksen, "Home Away from Home," *NRTA News Bulletin*, (Washington, D.C., April 1989), Vol. 30, No. 4, adapted from pp. 8,9.
2. Helene MacLean, *Caring for Your Parents* (New York: Doubleday, 1987), p. 213.
3. Update, "Paying for a Nursing Home," *Consumer Reports*, October, 1989, p. 664.
4. Florence D. Shelley and Jane Otten, *When Your Parents Grow Old*, (New York: Harper & Row, 1988).
5. Eugenia Anderson-Ellis and Marsha Dryan, *Aging Parents and You*, (New York: Master Media Limited, 1988), p. 178.

Chapter Nine

"I Shouldn't Feel This Way, But..."

Over and over I heard it. It became a familiar phrase punctuating so many of the conversations I had with adult children as we talked about their duties and responsibilities of caregiving. Most said it in an apologetic tone. Some assumed a defensive attitude as though they expected me to condemn. Others said it with indignation, while still others said it softly through their tears.

The unique fact was that the phrase always started with almost the same words. Only the middle and the end of the utterance were different. No matter how the phrase was delivered it was obvious that it came from the hearts of people who were hurting and confused and disappointed in themselves.

Attempts were made to avoid the expression, but sooner or later in our conversation that phrase would surface. "I know I shouldn't feel this way, BUT..." And then there were a variety of reasons why that person shouldn't feel that way—but did. The reasons were prefaced by such comments as, "When Mom (or Dad):

- is so irritable...
- is so demanding...
- expects me to spend so much time with her...
- acts so hurt when my husband and I fail to include him in *all* of our activities...
- refuses to do anything for himself even when able...

The end of the phrase, a phrase that has now become a sentence loaded with emotions and attitudes, ends with expressions of the speaker's feelings:

- I feel so angry! I have no time for *my* family or myself."
- I feel so guilty when I don't always take her with us."
- I feel so frustrated because I know I am being manipulated."

Can you identify with people who make these comments? Have *you* made comments that are similar? If so, welcome to the human race! Furthermore, if we are honest, I believe most of us will need to plead guilty.

People—parents and adult children—who are experiencing tremendous pressure due to circumstances resulting from illness, aging and caregiving are often caught in an avalanche of disturbing and sometimes frightening emotions. Frightening because, under the tension of handling our own families and responsibilities, we suddenly find ourselves feeling shocked at the disturbing emotions that surface toward the loved one for whom we must care.

In chapter 2 we dealt with some of the feelings and emotions of the elderly. In this chapter we want to center on some of the emotions the caregivers experience when parents are ill or have become bored, self-centered and demanding as a result of a lack of interest in other people or activities.

Whether we realize it or not, emotions are powerful forces within the human mind. Emotions have a surprising impact on human behavior. To bottle up

---

It is not surprising that anger is one of the most prevalent emotions with which caregivers struggle. Continuing demands become draining on the strongest person.

---

emotions such as resentment, hurt feelings, bitterness, extensive anger or hatred, extreme worry and fear, can have a devastating effect on our lives. How? By causing us to feel guilty or to feel like failures. Furthermore, repressed negative emotions can become some of the main contributors to feelings of burnout, fatigue or even illness.

Did you know, for example, that hatred burns up a large amount of energy? Professionals in the medical field report that *five minutes* of intensive hatred burns up more energy than *eight hours* of hard labor! Shocking, isn't it? Most caregivers do not have that much energy to spare!

As caregivers identified the emotions that were troubling them through the telling comment, "I shouldn't feel this way, but..." they most often mentioned anger first. Then came the feelings of guilt, depression, frustration at role-reversal, fear and loneliness. I could identify with these honest caregivers because, at times when my load seemed heavier than usual during my caregiving days, I struggled with some of the same emotions.

Those of us who grew up in Christian homes may tend to be a little too hard on ourselves in the adult child and parent relationship. Many of us have set a high standard for ourselves because we love, honor and respect our parents in obedience to the Word of God. When caregiving responsibilities become so heavy and are added to an already full daily schedule, we go into overload. That is often the time the "negative" emotions erupt.

I am so grateful that, while I was caring for my mother, I eventually found out that some of the struggles I had blamed on what I thought were my own weaknesses and inability to cope were, in reality, natural and very common. Prayer, waiting on the Lord, and being open to suggestions and guidance from some professionals were a great help to me.

I do not profess to be an authority to provide all of the answers. As we consider some of these emotions, I will attempt only to share some of the truths I learned. If you are suffering severe emotional trauma, you need to seek professional help. Talk to your doctor about finding the assistance you need. As lay people, let's consider some common emotions that frequently create problems for caregivers.

Anger

Before the days when you were involved in caregiving, under what circumstances did you find yourself becoming most irritable in your daily routine? For most people, irritability is the result of having too much to do and having too many demands being made on their time. They become irritable and angry when they are fatigued and worn out. That being true, it is not surprising that anger is one of the most prevalent emotions with which caregivers struggle. The continuing demands become draining on even the strongest person.

Unfortunately, the resulting anger may be directed toward a spouse, other family members or even at the illness of the care receiver and, through that channel, the patient becomes the object of anger. Caregivers may become very angry with themselves because they imagine they are not doing enough. They feel like failures. At times that anger is directed toward God—whether it is expressed or repressed. Questions begin to torment the weary caregiver: If God is loving, *why* does He permit my loved one to suffer? Closely following that *why* comes a tendency toward self-pity: Why am *I* tied down like this? Why do *I* have to be saddled with *all* of the responsibility? Where *is* God?

Carolyn and her mother were good friends. Both were active in their church as well as in their community. Carolyn's children loved spending time with their grandmother.

Carolyn remembers the day when she and her mother attended a funeral of an elderly lady from their church who died peacefully in her sleep. Her mother's comment was, "I hope when my time comes, I'll go quickly, too."

Later Carolyn's mother was diagnosed as having Alzheimers and was confined to an extended care facility. As Carolyn talked about her feelings she said, "To see her deteriorating before my eyes is heartbreaking!" said Carolyn, dabbing at her tears. "There are times when I am *so* angry with God! Mother doesn't deserve that! She has always been such a fine Christian, and now this...."

Carolyn's comments struck a responsive chord in my own heart. I remembered one weekend after my mother had been in a convalescent hospital more than seven years and, once again, had become deathly ill. She looked so tiny and vulnerable and had already been through so much. Mom was tired. She often asked, "Why doesn't the Lord take me home?"

That time was not yet to be. She improved slightly, and I was relieved; my emotions, however, were mixed. Along with gratitude for improvement, there was anger—hidden, but very real—at God. How long did Mom have to endure being so ill, improving for a time only to become deathly ill again? Hadn't she suffered enough? Where was God? My prayers seemed to go no higher than the ceiling.

A fellow worker, a godly man, sensed my problem and we began to talk. When at last I admitted my feelings he asked, "Have you told God that you're angry with Him?"

Of course I hadn't! His question brought me up short. I realized I was so angry I had not prayed for days. Yes, I knew better, but....My friend urged me to tell the Lord exactly how I felt. After he prayed, my friend's parting challenge was, "You know, Ruth, God knows every thought of your heart—so talk to Him about it!"

How often I had said those very words to others, but I had failed to practice them. I did talk very frankly to the Lord in the privacy of my home. What a relief when I realized I had been forgiven for allowing anger to break fellowship with Him. My situation did not change, but thanks to the Lord's mercy, compassion and love, my anger subsided and I could go on.

While not everyone experiences anger in the same way, you need to realize that anger is a normal reaction. It must not, however, be permitted to become a daily emotional pattern. Anger can lead to other destructive emotions for yourself, as well as guilt and regret when directed toward the care receiver.

The longer anger is left to simmer or kept repressed, the more bitter you will become. Recognize that the pressures and emotional strain of caring for a disabled person mean that there will be times when you will become angry. Instead of letting anger grow, or wallowing in self-pity or guilt, get help! No doubt part of the problem is that you need a break from your daily routine. Perhaps a friend or relative can help out so you can have time for yourself. Above all, don't bottle up the anger—that only leads to more complex problems. Remember, "In your anger do not sin, do not let the sun go down while you are still angry, and do not give the devil a foothold."[1] So talk to someone who is not directly involved in your situation—like your pastor, for example. If necessary, find a counselor who can help you sort out your emotions and discover some of the reasons—aside from an obvious over-load—that are feeding your anger.

It is surprising what just an hour to yourself can do to restore frazzled emotions. Meet a friend and play a game of tennis, go for a walk or go swimming. Healthy, strenuous exercise is an excellent remedy for tension. Or pamper yourself and make an appointment to get your hair and nails done.

Every caregiver needs a place to be alone for a time, whether it is a place in the basement, your own room, a park, or simply a favorite chair where you can put up your feet for an hour and relax. If you feel ready to burst into tears, go to your room and have a good cry, or do some reading. The Psalms can be a real balm for frayed nerves—they were for me. Or just sit quietly and recall some of the blessings God has showered upon you in the past, and then praise Him. Listen to some of your favorite music. After an hour of quietness, you will find your world can look completely different. Getting away for short times is a *must* for each day of your busy schedule.

Guilt

Following closely on the heels of anger is the feeling of guilt. The very nature of caregiving involves guilt-producing actions, as adult children need to assist their parents with such personal needs that appear to strip the dignity from the oldster. In the past our parents have been strong, independent, available to us when we had a need. Therefore, when it becomes necessary for an adult child to clean a parent's dentures or to bathe a parent, the child feels guilty for being put into that role of giving care. Author Tim Stafford says that the resulting emotions from such assistance include both guilt and anger. The only person who does not feel guilt, says Stafford, is "a child with a very poor sense of responsibility toward his parents. All others will feel guilty."[2]

Guilt-producing questions for the adult child can be endless: Why did I yell at her when she's so vulnerable? Should I spend more time with him? Am I being selfish? Have I done everything I can to help him? Should we have put her in a nursing home? Could we have managed in a better way?

Notice that the above examples of guilt-producing questions are all directed toward self. Guilt usually cancels feelings of self-worth and blames self. Anger may blame others for a problem, but guilt often says, "I'm no good. I should have done more. I hate myself." Yes, guilt is a devastating emotion that can result in ruining your life if it goes unchecked.

In the most unexpected situations guilt sneaks up on the adult child even when a parent is not disabled. Recall the case of Bob and his mother, Mabel, mentioned in chapter 4. Mabel lived alone and was quite independent, but her requests and attitude produced guilt feelings in Bob when he failed to include her in their family vacation.

God's original plan was, "A man will leave his father and mother and be united to his wife, and they will become one flesh."[3] A counselor would no doubt have told Bob that, at times, it is okay to say no to a demanding parent. Bob had provided for Mabel, and he had a responsibility to his own family. There was, therefore, no reason for him to feel guilt as he fulfilled his responsibility to his own wife and children.

Consider the case of Norman. His aged father was

in a nursing home when Norman's company transferred him to a neighboring state. The move meant
uprooting his family, but the new job was an excellent
advancement despite the added pressure and responsibility. Norman faced the stress of a new job, the emotional upheaval of the family finding new friends, new
schools, a new church *and* the big question of what to
do about his father. No other relatives were nearby to
care for the older man.

Norman and his wife prayed for guidance. Should
they move his father? They consulted with the doctor
and were assured that moving the older man was possible.

After much thought and prayer, Norman made
arrangements to have his father flown to a nursing
home in their new hometown. Although the doctor
had sedated the patient before take-off, the sedative
seemed to wear off as they gained altitude. The rest-
lessness of his father during the flight was devastating
to Norman. To make matters worse, the older man
died soon after the move, leaving his son to suffer
overwhelming guilt and anger. There was no evidence
that the move was responsible for his father's death.
Nevertheless, Norman was haunted by guilt and fear:
If only he had not moved his father, perhaps he would
not have died. If only he had not changed jobs! Was it
a mistake? Should he have declined the promotion?

Caregivers need to recognize that there is authentic guilt and false guilt. Authentic guilt comes from a
heart conviction based on God's Word, which points
out the sin and wrongdoing in our lives. False guilt is
just that—false. It becomes a tool of self-punishment
as victims nurse imagined or real failures, and blows
the problems out of proportion. Both men, Bob and

Norman, did the best they knew how to solve their problems under the circumstances facing them.

Caregivers—even the best ones—are human and, therefore, subject to failure and error. Unless you have never made an error in other areas of your life, you will no doubt make a few errors and a few poor decisions in caregiving. Don't set your standards so high that you expect perfection from yourself, because if you do you are riding for a fall.

False guilt can entrap caregivers with something as simple as taking, or failing to take, a badly needed respite. I dreaded vacations while my mother was confined. My doctor and my family insisted that I must get away. Mentally, I knew they were right, but each year I felt the same trauma as I faced a week of vacation. I knew that under normal circumstances Mom would have insisted I go, but I still felt guilty. I did get away, but it took several days to relax and stop mentally living through the hours of the day with her.

Coping with Guilt

To cope with false or authentic guilt you need to take a realistic look at your situation. Have a counselor, a pastor or knowledgeable friend help you sort out your feelings and evaluate your caregiving. Are your expectations of the role realistic? Can you really expect more of yourself?

Most likely you will have to admit that you are doing your best under the circumstances. If so, recognize that a large part of your problem is false guilt. And if under pressure you blew it and lost your cool, your loved one isn't going to die because you did. If, in fact, you have truly neglected or wronged your parent, you can find forgiveness by confessing that wrong to the Lord.[4] After He forgives, the Lord often uses our failures as a positive influence for good in our lives.[5] Basing your conviction on God's Word, believe that He has forgiven you. Believe also that, when God forgives, He also forgets;[6] therefore, you too may forget it. Ask the Lord to help you direct your thought pattern as instructed in His Word.[7]

Finally, forgive yourself and stop torturing yourself with the "what ifs" or the "I should haves." Since the Lord has so graciously forgiven you, for goodness sakes, don't pick up your guilty load again! You have been invited to "Cast all your anxiety on [Jesus Christ] because he cares for you."[8] Who can refuse an invitation like that?

Frustrations of Role Reversal

Role reversal involves both responsibilities and roles; therefore, we need to define roles. The word "role" describes *who* a person is in a family, while "responsibility" defines the *tasks* performed in that specific role. In the past the father's role was defined as the head of the household, the breadwinner. The role of the married woman was to become a homemaker, taking care of matters pertaining to running the home. As her role expanded to include motherhood, she assumed the responsibility of nurturing and caring for the children. These roles, of course, have changed in our culture today.

Illness and aging usually mean that roles and responsibilities also change. When an adult child must take over some of the tasks from an aging parent, it is usually difficult for both parent and child. This take-over *does not* mean the parent becomes a child, even when there is childlike behavior due to diseases such as Alzheimer's disease or related dementing illnesses. Disabled parents are not being taught something new; they are being helped with functions such as feeding or changing clothes because the aging process has taken its toll. A better definition of the change may be a *shift* in roles and responsibilities, rather than role reversal, as the child gradually assumes more responsibilities for the parent.

To give up performing one's own personal tasks destroys self-dignity and often creates resentment. Remember, part of the fear of the elderly is losing independence. They want to be in charge of their own lives as long as possible. Children who recognize and respect that need will allow parents to maintain their dignity even when help is definitely needed. How? By simply *asking* for permission to help—to get the mail, do the laundry, the cleaning or the banking. Granting permission allows the parent to feel that he or she is still in charge. It can also turn a potential act of intrusion into a loving gesture of care and concern.

Role changes are often difficult. We hate to witness losses in a loved one. The adult child usually experiences sadness and guilt in assuming more responsibilities. At the same time, parents see their independence, leadership and responsibilities disappear, and often become discouraged, depressed or argumentative.

The way a parent responds to a new role depends largely on the role held before disability. If child and parent are able to communicate—to talk *and listen* to each other—role reversal will be much smoother. Having a voice in decision making allows the parent to retain feelings of self-worth and respect.

169

Not all parents and children have enjoyed good relationships. Some adult children are still dependent on their parents, perhaps because the apron strings were never cut. When those parents become ill, the child often feels trapped and blames the parent for being demanding and manipulative. At the same time, the parent may insist that, despite any disabilities, he or she can manage alone if "you'll just lend a hand now and then." In reality, instead of helping "now and then," the child must spend many hours each week assisting and caring for a disabled parent. The end result is a real conflict because expectations of child and parent are miles apart. Fortunately, most families have adjusted to role reversal by facing their problems. As a result they have been drawn closer together than ever before.

The caregiver responsible for a spouse will also experience changes in roles. If both husband and wife are still able to enjoy a measure of good health, now is the time to learn as much as possible about each other's responsibilities. Learning how to do the laundry now—even if it has always been *her* job—will keep you from wearing pale pink socks and shorts later. If your spouse has always managed the finances, insist that you both know about all pensions, stocks, bonds, IRAs, mortgages and debts. Do you both know about the will and where it is kept? Grief, when disability or death comes, is traumatic enough without the added burden of assuming unfamiliar roles and responsibilities.

Fear, Loneliness, Depression

Once the caregiver has begun the daily routine of caregiving, it may quickly be discovered that the load is far more than anticipated. That is when the emotions of fear, loneliness and depression often become the caregiver's companions. There is the fear of not being able to continue as long as necessary. Or the fear that the illness may be hereditary. Such fears are common. If these fears begin to snowball, the caregiver should consider talking to a counselor, a pastor or a support group. An outside contact can help take away that lonely feeling most caregivers have.

If you feel lonely, remember that you are not alone. The Lord has promised never to leave His own. Spend much time in prayer and with other Christians in Bible study. Continue to attend worship services. If you do not know how to have a close personal fellowship with the Lord, contact a Bible teaching church and ask the pastor to show you the way.

When a caregiver experiences depression, that is the time for a break. Ask another family member or a friend to relieve you for a weekend. Or contact the health care services in your area—such as a day care center—that may be able to take your parent for a day or two.

Uncontrolled Emotions

We could go on for some time listing other emotions that contribute to problems for caregivers. One important concern relating to the pressure and heavy responsibility of caregiving is one we dare not overlook. That concern is to urge all caregivers to get help if there is danger of losing control. Uncontrolled emotions lead to greater problems and, sometimes, to abuse of the elderly. As in other cases of family and/or child abuse, however, there really is no one cause for the great sin of abusing the defenseless.

Are you aware that abuse of the elderly is a full-scale national problem in America? According to the House Select Committee on Aging, about 4 percent of our nation's elderly may be victims of some kind of abuse, ranging from moderate to severe. The Committee further reported that 1.1 million older Americans may be victims of abuse every year. To break down these statistics, one out of every twenty-five elderly Americans is abused.[9]

The Committee on Aging indicated that the figures are, perhaps, even higher because they are based on cases *reported* to social service agencies. Only one out of six cases come to the attention of the authorities, however. Fear, shame and a feeling that they are the cause of the abuse keep most elderly victims from reporting the abuse they experience.[10]

These figures were shocking to me and, in an interview with family counselor Dr. Judith Alexandre, I asked if she ever found abuse of the elderly among Christian families. Her answer surprised me. Without hesitation she said, "Oh yes, even in Christian families!"

Hard as it is to believe, abuse of the elderly crops up everywhere—in cities, towns, suburbs and rural areas, and in all classes of society.

In his book on family violence and abuse, Dr. Grant L. Martin, psychologist and family therapist, mentions four categories of abuse: physical, psychological, material and medical.[11]

The average person is repulsed at the thought of vulnerable, aging people being victims of bodily injuries inflicted upon them or being mistreated by unreasonable restraints or confinements. Unfortunately, while physical abuse is sickening, people who recoil at the thought of physical abuse often do not realize the pain the elderly suffer from psychological abuse, which includes verbal assaults, ridicule, threats or insults. Yet, adult children have been known to work out their frustration on the elderly in these forms of abuse.

Some adult children assume that, because the elderly have limited hearing and eyesight, or since their aged bodies no longer move as rapidly as they once did, feelings and emotions have also deteriorated. Not so. To be abused physically or psychologically is devastating and painful, regardless of age. The elders have not become non-persons as a result of aging.

Dr. Martin's definition of material abuse includes cheating the elderly out of personal benefits, monetary gains and resources they have accumulated to meet their retirement needs. This abuse is done illegally, of course, and often through force or misrepresentation.[12]

A Healthy Emotion

Family violence and abuse of the elderly is a truth that must not be covered up, but I do not want to end this chapter without a brighter picture of caregiving. Caregiving is not all doom and gloom. You will experience great times of joy, as well. Joy comes as you and your parent relive favorite memories. It can come if you maintain a good sense of humor and do not take yourself too seriously. Joy can come as you share your favorite psalm or other passages from the Bible, and remember God's faithfulness in the past—as well as in

173

the present. Talk with the care receiver. Don't be afraid to honestly express your feelings while encouraging him or her to do the same. Both of you will be the better for it.

You have the right to feel you are doing something wonderful as you give care to someone who needs it. This was a truth I had to learn because I always felt a bit embarrassed when people would comment about God rewarding me for taking care of my mother. I didn't want any rewards—I just wanted her to be comfortable and happy. Nevertheless, the attitude of the caregiver is very important, especially if it is an attitude of love and warmhearted giving. The Bible says, "I assure you that whatever you did for the humblest of my brothers you did for me."[13]

Notes

1. Ephesians 4:26,27.
2. Tim Stafford, *As Our Years Increase* (Grand Rapids: Zondervan Publishing House, 1989), p. 143.
3. Genesis 2:24.
4. 1 John 1:9.
5. Romans 8:28.
6. Hebrews 10:17,18.
7. Philippians 4:8.
8. 1 Peter 5:7.
9. Select Committee on Aging, "Elder Abuse: A National Disgrace, Introduction and Executive Summary," *Caring* (January 1986), pp. 5-7.
10. Ibid.
11. Grant L. Martin, *Counseling for Family Violence and Abuse* (Waco: Word Books, 1987), Volume 6 of the Resources for Christian Counseling Series, adapted from p. 244.
12. Ibid.
13. Matthew 25:40, *Phillips*.

Chapter Ten
Selecting a Nursing Home

Have you noticed the clever game of words advertisers use to sell their products? Usually an appeal is made to the consumer's self-image or to the ego as the buyer is flattered with such labels as "a wise shopper," "a person of distinction," or "the sophisticated buyer." Having built up a prospective consumer to purchase a piece of jewelry, for example, the buyer then needs to know why she (being the "person of distinction" that she is!) dare not deny herself ownership. Then comes the bottom line: "This can be yours for ONLY $1,495!" That little word "only" sounds good, but that amount of money is a lot for a piece of jewelry, especially for the average wage earner.

Automobile manufacturers play the game by labeling their latest models with a long list of intriguing names, including Jaguar, Cougar, Eagle or Lark, to list just a few.

Owners of nursing homes have also seized the use of this gimmick. At one time, institutions for extended care for the elderly were known by such common names as "Rest Home" or "Old Folks Home." Currently, those two names have all but disappeared, perhaps because of the unfavorable connotations often associated with those labels. Today nursing home names have been changed to such friendly, attractive labels as "Sunshine Manor," "Blue Lake Guest Home," or "Twin Oak Acres." Unfortunately, changing the name has not necessarily changed the facilities nor the concept the elderly and their families have of them.

Most caregivers tend to care for their loved ones at home long after the care receiver should have been placed into a nursing home. Experts in the field report that this lengthy care is more prevalent when the caregiver is a spouse or a close family member.

My father was ill with cancer for five years before he died. With the exception of two confinements in an acute care hospital for surgery, my mother, then in her mid-sixties, cared for him at home. Years later, when she needed care after surgery, there was no choice for us. I had a full-time job and Mom needed around-the-clock nursing care. Much as I disliked the idea, the doctor ordered her moved to an extended care facility. The only thing that made the move a little easier for me was that the decision was not really up to us—the doctor made it for us. Our choice was to select the facility—a bewildering choice, at best.

Nursing Home Trauma

For many families, finding a nursing home and moving a loved one into that facility can be one of the toughest decisions they will ever make. That decision becomes a traumatic experience for several reasons.

First, we don't like the idea of long-term care, even

when we admit the need for it. Our society has become accustomed to getting things done in a hurry. We have instant food, microwave ovens, automatic bank tellers and overnight express mail. To see a loved one incapacitated for more than a few days is frustrating and painful because extended disability is contrary to our mode of rushing through life.

One very busy daughter summed up the problem this way: "I hated to see my father so fragile. I just wanted him to bounce back and become his old self again. I needed to get on with my own life and career. I always felt mature and secure in thinking I could handle whatever life handed me—until I saw my once strong father change almost overnight after his stroke."

Perhaps your parents, like many elderly, have always insisted they would never consent to living in a nursing home. In that case, when a decision for an extended care facility must be made, the adult child is frequently plagued with feelings of disobedience, of breaking a promise of long standing. One man told me through his tears that, after he moved his father into a nursing home, the older man quietly said, "Son, I didn't think you would ever do this to me!"

For me, as well as for many adult children, there was a period of deep grief that came with moving my mother into a convalescent hospital.

A second reason families sometimes experience the nursing home trauma is that the decision and need for finding a facility often comes during a crisis. Patients who have suffered a catastrophic illness often are discharged from an acute care hospital when the family (due to a lack of medical knowledge) feels that the patient still appears to be far too ill to be moved.

177

The family has not had sufficient time to recover from all the emotions involved in the trauma of a loved one having a stroke or a heart attack and being rushed to an acute care hospital. Witnessing their loved one in pain has upset the entire family. While still rather numb from the initial crisis, the family is suddenly confronted with locating another care facili-

The more time you have to search for a nursing home, the more you will be satisfied with your final choice.

ty, moving an ailing parent and completing a myriad of necessary questionnaires.

A third reason for the trauma is that many adult children are not ready to admit to themselves that the time has come to release a parent to a nursing home. This is often the time the caregiver is overwhelmed with guilt and a sense of failure and inadequacy. Many adult children have admitted feeling angry at themselves when their parent went into a nursing home. Why? Because they felt they were deserting their parent just when that ill, frail loved one needed the child most.

Other factors, of course, contribute to the trauma of moving a loved one into a nursing home, but the above three are some of the more basic a family may face. We need to remember that the emotional upheaval not only affects the caregiver and family members. If the care receiver is mentally aware of what is happening, that person will have numerous concerns. In the next chapter we will discuss ways of making that move as easy as possible.

Advance preparation in finding a nursing home may soften the emotional decision somewhat. If your parent has a chronic or progressive illness or mental disorder indicating inevitable extended care in the near future, it is wise to begin to investigate possible facilities in your area *before* that care is actually needed. The reason for this long-range plan is a deplorable shortage of beds available. Statistics indicate that 90 percent of nursing home beds are filled at any given time.[1] Most of the better facilities have a long waiting list. It is therefore important for the caregiver to have a well-planned strategy of possible options before a crisis arises.

The more time you have to search for a nursing home, the more you will be satisfied with your final choice because you will have had time to consider all of the alternatives. If the nursing home has a bed available before your parent needs it, explain that you are not ready yet, but ask to remain on their preferential waiting list. Depending on your circumstances, you could agree to give the home as much notice as possible before you are ready to have your parent moved into the facility. The home will appreciate your attitude and will no doubt try to work with you.

We need to recognize that moving a loved one into a nursing home is never easy, but when that decision must be faced, the family—after prayer and often with the help of their doctor—must decide what is best for the care receiver. And when extended care is clearly the best decision under the circumstances, it is time to try to put aside fears, trust in the Lord's leading and make the best arrangements possible. If a parent is mentally competent, he or she should definitely be included in the discussions, the decision and even the arrangements for moving into a nursing home. To ignore a parent while making all the necessary arrangements and then announce a final decision to move, only creates problems and more heartaches. Professional counseling may be helpful for both caregiver and parent facing a move into a nursing home.

Is It Time for the Move?

Older people want to live the way they are accustomed to living—in their own home, with their own possessions, answering to no one. And as we have already indicated, independent living is important for the elderly and should be permitted and encouraged as long as possible.

All too often in the aging process, all other independent or semi-independent living arrangements for the elderly eventually become an impossibility. It is then that the next step must be taken—moving a disabled loved one into a nursing home. Seldom is this option chosen unless there is an order from a doctor or there is absolutely no other choice. Even then it is frequently done out of a deep sense of desperation. The big question still is: When is the move to a nursing home the next step? If, after a long period of caregiving, you are asking that question, it is well for you to consider the following signs. It is time for a nursing home when:

1. The care receiver's condition has progressively worsened. At times the elderly becomes violent, hostile, extremely senile or incontinent.
2. Care duties have multiplied to the point where home responsibilities are being neglected, including spouse and children.
3. The care receiver's illness now requires turning, moving and lifting the patient. These duties are taxing your physical strength beyond your ability.
4. You are often irritable and exhausted because there is no time for other interests.
5. You, the caregiver, become ill or have more symptoms of possible illness than before caring for your loved one.[2]

The Search for a Facility

The different types of extended care facilities were discussed in chapter 8. Usually your doctor will recommend the type of nursing home your parent will need. If the doctor fails to do so and you are uncertain, ask the doctor for guidance.

How does one begin the search for a nursing home? Start by asking advice. Doctors, especially general practitioners (GPs) visit many nursing homes and are acquainted with the facilities in your community. Your doctor, like mine, may be hesitant to recommend one specific facility; but many GPs will give guidance, especially if they have known the family for a time. Or call the County Nursing Home Referral in your community. The phone number is in your telephone directory.

Talk to visiting nurses, ministers (who frequently visit the elderly) and family friends who already have a loved one in a nursing home. Another excellent source for information are the social workers found in most acute care hospitals. Just ask for the hospital social service department. These workers often have the inside information concerning staff, as well as operation of nursing homes.

Contact local organizations listed in your telephone directory, such as the Area Agency on Aging, the Bureau of Long-Term Care and the American Association of Homes for the Aging. If you are not in a crisis situation when you need a nursing home, you may write to some of the addresses listed below and secure any helpful brochures available. (The American Health Care Association has a helpful pamphlet entitled "Thinking About a Nursing Home?")

The American Health Care Association
1200 15th Street N.W.
Washington, D.C. 20005

U.S. Department of Health and Human Services
Public Health Service,
Office of Nursing Home Affairs
5600 Fisher Lane
Rockville, MD 20858

The American Association of Homes
for the Aging
1129 20th Street, N.W., Suite 400
Washington, D.C. 20036
202/296-5960

Nursing Home Information Service
925 15th St., N.W.
Washington, D.C. 20005
202/347-8800

In your search for a nursing home, whether it is for a need in the future or an immediate need in a time of crisis, it is well to gather pertinent information from all facilities you visit. Carry a looseleaf notebook or set up several file folders. Write down such information as names of administrators, owners (if privately owned), phone numbers, general impressions, Medicare-Medicaid information and information on staff.

Licensed Homes

Are you aware that all state governments require nursing homes to be licensed? Each facility must comply with specific standards established by a licensing agency for acceptable business practices as well as acceptable levels of patient care. Although regulations differ in various states, it is through licensing that the consumer is protected.

At least once a year the state government must inspect all facilities to determine whether the nursing home meets federal standards. Only after the state certifies that the nursing home has met the required standards for that year will the federal government renew the facility's Medicare-Medicaid contract. If a facility is not licensed by the state in which it is located, it also is ineligible to receive federal certification for Medicare or Medicaid benefits.

A list of licensed nursing homes is available at your public library. You may also secure a list from your local Social Security office, the local department on aging or the state Welfare Office.

The Ombudsman Program

I wish I had known about the Ombudsman program while my mother was in an extended care facility. This program is a great help to the elderly. In 1978 the Older American Act of 1965 was amended to include the establishment of a long-term care Ombudsman program for each state. The program is administered through your local State Department of Aging.

The best description of Ombudsman is to say it is a watchdog program established to protect the rights of all residents of nursing homes and other extended care facilities. According to their own literature, the Ombudsman personnel answer questions, provide pre-admission counseling to the elderly and their families, as well as information and referral about long-term care. Nursing home residents and/or family members may report any care-related problems in confidence to Ombudsman without fear of reprisal. Volunteers who regularly visit nursing homes will follow up on the complaints and attempt to resolve the problem. In other words, the Ombudsman program serves as a resident advocate between nursing home residents and the facility. If necessary, the program will even assist residents in getting legal help. An important goal of the Ombudsman program is to improve the quality of life for long-term residents. You can find the phone number for your local Ombudsman program in your telephone directory.

I feel confident you will find Ombudsman most helpful. Some years ago I visited Pearl, a mentally sharp, alert ninety-eight-year-old resident in a long-term facility in Ventura, California. Communication with her was next to impossible because Pearl was almost deaf and an ordinary hearing aid was ineffective. It was sad because she wanted so desperately to know what was going on in the world, and often wanted me to read the newspaper and other magazines to her. Have you ever shouted your way through a news article? It's not easy!

One day when I arrived, Pearl was very excited. Her doctor had brought in a new hearing device that he wanted her to try. To communicate with her, one had to speak into a small hand microphone that was somehow connected to a hearing aid she wore. We had a wonderful visit and she was thrilled as she was able to hear the articles I read to her.

Later on, however, I frequently discovered the hearing device in a drawer where Pearl either could not find it or could not reach it. On one visit I discovered the device jammed into a drawer with other items and buried in chocolate candy! On still another visit when Pearl was again without the device, I asked the charge nurse about it. I was told it was at the nurses' station where it had been for a week because they had not yet gotten around to ordering batteries for it.

It was frustrating to see Pearl unnecessarily cut off from others due to hearing impairment when a hearing device was available. In an attempt to help I called the Ombudsman office in our city. Despite the fact that I was not a family member, I was pleased to see how quickly an Ombudsman volunteer followed up on the complaint.

Visit and Evaluate Homes

Assuming you have a list of several available nursing homes gathered from the sources suggested in this chapter, you are now ready for the next step—visiting the facilities on your list. Plan to visit several nursing homes before making any final decision. Also, plan to make at least two visits to any facility that appears to be promising.

You can save time and energy by using your telephone to discover important basic information before your first visit. Again, a looseleaf notebook with the following questions listed and space for answers will be helpful in securing accurate information from each facility. You will want to know: (1) Is the facility currently accepting new residents? (2) If not, is there a waiting list? How long is the list? (3) What level of care is provided? (4) What is their Medicare policy? Will they allow a person to stay on if financial resources diminish and the patient becomes dependent on Medicaid (welfare)?

Unfortunately, as with most every other decision in life, the financial problem will without a doubt influence the selection of a nursing home. The annual costs are very high. In 1988 the average cost for a year in a nursing home was $22,000 or more. That figure is estimated to more than double by the year 2018 to about $55,000 by the year 2018 if inflation continues at a moderate rate.[3]

In your exploration for a nursing home you will need to be sure that you and your parent clearly understand what, if any, Medicare benefits are available. See chapter 8 for the limitations for this government insurance coverage. Also, check with your local Medicare office.

Contrary to popular belief, many homes do not accept persons who are unable to pay for at least a portion of the cost. Justified or not, many homes will not accept your parent if he or she is dependent on Medicare funds from the date of admittance. And even with Medicare many families have been disappointed to discover how much of the cost reverts back to the elderly or to the family. Benefits and laws governing Medicare and Medicaid change; therefore, you need to be informed of the current benefits. You will quickly discover that private nursing homes are even more costly. In fact, without some government subsidies, even comparatively wealthy families have experienced great financial difficulties. If, however, money is not a problem, the privately owned homes may be the way you want to go.

Your next step in your search for a nursing home is to set up an appointment with the director/administrator of prospective nursing homes on your list for your first visit.

The Initial Shock

Never will I forget some of my first impressions when we visited some of the facilities for my mother. Not only were we rushed for time, but to me it was a painful, bewildering and frightening experience. The sounds, the unpleasant odors in some facilities, the crowded corridors jammed with wheelchairs, walkers and people in apparent various degrees of mental stability caused my stomach to tie up in knots. I wanted to bolt and run. Racing through my mind was a silent scream, "My mother doesn't belong here!" I had been expecting an atmosphere of an acute care hospital, and this was far from my expectations.

I have since discovered that my first impressions were not unique. That is why I am sharing them here, so that perhaps by being forewarned your shock may be a little less traumatic than mine. Gerontologists tell me that my reactions to those first visits are actually very common for a novice visitor to a nursing home. The average person is not well acquainted with the population and functions of a nursing home, so it is similar to a journey into the unknown. Try not to become too discouraged after your first few visits. Once I got over my initial shock I was finally able to see that many of the residents were actually participating in activities and were obviously enjoying themselves.

Tour Before Choosing a Home

When you make your initial phone call for an appointment, be sure to clearly request that you be given a tour of the facility. Be specific as to the areas you want to see. Include a visit to the therapy sessions, the recreation activities, the kitchen, meal service and some of the residents' rooms. Ask the administrator to suggest the best time of the day for you to visit so that you might see these areas. Most homes suggest mid-morning, after breakfast is out of the way and the patients have been cleaned up.

On your first visit you should meet the administrator or director. Do not hesitate to ask to see the nursing home's state license. That is your right. Take note of the date to be certain the license is current. Every nursing home is required by federal regulations to display the Declaration of Patient's Rights in a conspicuous place—most have the document in the entry way. If you do not see it, ask for it.

Ask the administrator for a copy of the admission contract, which patients are required to sign before being admitted as a resident. Never sign this contract until you have thoroughly read it. You may want a lawyer to go over it with you. The better informed you are, the less the possibility of future problems. Even though you plan to visit several facilities, it is well to secure admission contracts from each.

Karen Horlick, director of social services at California Medical Center, is quoted as encouraging families touring nursing homes not to be misled by those first appearances. Ms. Horlick says that some of the homes that appear to be the best have been known for the most questionable care, while some of the plainest

---

You have a right to know all about the facility you are visiting because it is your parent and your finances that are involved.

---

nursing homes gave the best care.[4]

You have a right to know all about the facility you are visiting because it is your parent and your finances that are involved. The way you are received by the staff and administrator on your first visit is important: Do you sense an open, friendly, concerned attitude or are the personnel disgruntled and rather defensive, making you feel it is an imposition to have you request a tour? If the latter is true you may want to terminate your visit without completing an extensive tour.

Questions to Ask

Before you visit it is helpful to make a list of basic questions to help you make a better comparison between the facilities you visit and to help you evaluate each nursing home. You may have other questions, but the following are some you definitely need to consider.[5]

The Facility

- Is the place located near your home so that visits are convenient?
- Is there a vacancy? A long waiting list?
- Is it nonprofit or a for-profit facility?
- Is it approved for Medicaid-Medicare reimbursement?
- Is its license current?
- What is the basic cost? What, if any, are the extra charges? Does the basic cost include personal laundry, grooming and medical supplies?

The Building

- Check for safety. Are there handrails in hallways? Are there ramps for wheelchairs?
- Grab bars in bathrooms? Call bells in bathrooms and guest rooms?
- Are there smoke detectors and fire extinguishers evident throughout the building?
- What is the general atmosphere? Are rooms light and cheerful? Well ventilated? Is there an overbearing odor problem?
- Are hallways crowded or are there areas where residents may go for reading, watching television, etc.?
- Is there a home-like atmosphere or is it repressive?
- Is there a place for worship? Is there a visiting chaplain? Are churches within the area encouraged/permitted to come in to conduct religious services?

190

The Staff

- Is there a physician on staff or on call? (California law requires a doctor to visit his patient once a month.)
- What is the ratio of registered nurses (RNs) and LVNs to patients?
- What is the ratio of aides and/or orderlies to patients?
- Are medical consultants on staff or on call for dental, eye and foot care?
- Are physical therapists and/or social workers on staff?
- How are patient emergencies handled?
- As you walk through the halls, be alert to the way the staff treats residents. Are residents treated with respect and as the adults they are, or as children?
- Is there a trained activities director on staff? What type of activities are available? Is there a calendar of activities on display? Is the calendar current, or at least no older than one month?
- Does a nutritionist prepare meals? How much time is allowed for meals? What hours are meals served?
- What provision is made for patients who need to be hand-fed? Who feeds these patients?
- Ask to see a copy of the week's menu. Is there variety?
- What is the general appearance of the kitchen and staff?

Residents

- Do residents appear well groomed and cared for?
- Are the men shaved? Are hands and hair clean?
- Are residents out of their rooms and alert?
- How often are residents involved in activities?

- Are there areas where, weather permitting, residents may be outdoors?
- What belongings may be brought into the facility to make the residents feel at home?
- Do residents who show an interest have access to tapes and large print reading materials?

You will quickly discover that not every nursing home will rate an affirmative answer to each of the above questions. These questions are merely a guide to assist you in your evaluation.

Your overall goal in selecting a nursing home is to provide the best possible facility for your parent. However, there will be many contributing factors involved in that final decision. The best facilities are often the most expensive and the ones that most often have no vacancies. Many times, because of high costs and family finances, it may be necessary to choose a home that does not quite meet your standards. In his book, author Tim Stafford indicated that the most important concern in selecting the proper nursing home is probably the quality of the staff and administration. "Good people," said Stafford, "can make almost any facility work."[6] I am inclined to agree with his assessment.

Notes
1. Eugenia Anderson-Ellis and Marsha Dryan, *Aging Parents and You*, (New York: Master Media Limited, 1988), p. 215.
2. Jo Horne, *Helping an Aged Loved One*, (Glenview, IL: Scott, Foresman & Co., 1985), adapted from p. 283.
3. *Consumer Reports*, "Who Can Afford a Nursing Home?", May 1988, Vol. 53, No. 5, p. 300.
4. Barbara Bronson Gray, "How to Select the Nursing Home that Will Best Fill Your Needs," *Los Angeles Herald Examiner*, (August 19, 1986), C7.
5. Helene MacLean, *Caring for Your Parents*, (New York: Doubleday, 1987), adapted from pp. 231-233.
6. Tim Stafford, *As Our Years Increase*, (Grand Rapids: Zondervan Publishing House, 1989), p. 203.

Chapter Eleven

Moving into a Nursing Home

A friend of mine had her elderly mother in Elms Manor, a small, beautiful nursing home in our city that was owned and operated by the Presbyterian denomination. My friend had nothing but praise for the staff and the facility. The director of nurses was a registered nurse who had a sincere love and a deep concern for the comfort and welfare of the aged. Long before my mother became ill I had always hoped that, should a need arise for an extended care facility in our family, that home would be the one for us.

While Mom was still very ill in an acute care hospital after her surgery and with a poor prognosis, my Aunt Alma and I visited Elms Manor. The nursing home was all we had expected. The director and Aunt Alma, both of whom had devoted their adult lives to nursing, were soon chatting like old friends as they discussed the care older people needed. With my favorite aunt's stamp of approval on the facility, I felt much more at ease in the event we needed to eventually move my mother into a nursing home.

About three weeks later, when I was told my mother was to be released from the acute care hospital, I called Elms Manor. Much to my regret I was told there was no vacancy, and there was a long waiting list. Two of my brothers and I combed our city for another facility. Although Mom was mentally alert, she was far too ill to have much of a voice in the decision—it was up to us. I didn't realize what a novice I was at the time. We needed to find a bed for Mom within a day or two, and that was our main objective. Of course, we wanted the best for her, but we were frightened and had no idea of how to go about finding a facility.

After several rejections—either we were rejected or we rejected the facility for various reasons—we found a small convalescent hospital. To our inexperienced knowledge the place appeared to be okay. We felt Mom would receive better care because it was small and the staff would have more time for individual patient care—or so we thought. There *was* a vacancy, time *was* running out for us, so without checking any further we agreed this was the place.

That was the biggest mistake we could have made. Without personal know-how, and lacking any kind of professional guidance, we made a very poor choice. Within a few days I regretted the moment we walked into that facility. Nevertheless, we all survived and were able to correct our error. More about that later.

The Final Decision

Unlike our experience, when or if you are faced with moving a loved one into a nursing home, you will hopefully have more time to collect all the relevant information mentioned in the previous chapter. Unfortunately, however, most families do not have the luxury of preparing for a carefully, well-planned move unless the loved one has a chronic illness. Most families, like ours, usually are confronted with a speedy transfer directly from an acute care hospital to a nursing home.

Regardless of your situation, whether a rushed or a well planned move, you need to collect as much relevant information as possible before making that final decision of selecting an appropriate facility. When you have narrowed your choice of facilities down to several homes, talk to a professional—a social worker or someone from Ombudsman—about your choice. Often these persons have access to a rating list of nursing homes.

You may find that none of the places you have considered and/or visitied is completely to your liking and satisfaction. There are usually pros and cons in each facility that need to be carefully considered. If you feel you just cannot decide, you need to recognize that one reason for your hesitant decision may well be your emotional state. You are perhaps rejecting each facility because, subconsciously, you dislike the idea of a nursing home for your parent. Remember, however, that feelings of guilt, anxiety and doubt are common for families in your situation. Each caregiver must eventually come to accept the fact that when a parent becomes ill or very disabled the caregiving role expands. With the move into a nursing home there is no longer the intimate caregiver-parent situation. Now the scenario has expanded to include three in the care involvement: the nursing home staff, your parent and you—the caregiver. After Mom entered an extended care facility, I did not like to relinquish care responsibility to another, despite the fact that I knew we had no other choice.

Instead of dwelling on your own negative emotions, direct your attention to your parents. Our parents have heard all the unhappy stories associated with nursing homes, just as we have. Perhaps the ones they remember best are the accounts of parents who were admitted to nursing homes and then forgotten by family and friends. Moving into a nursing home, therefore, can be very traumatic. Coupled with the fear of the unknown, the move frequently represents yet another tremendous loss. Added to a series of losses already experienced in recent years, including the loss of mobility as a result of being deprived of driving privileges or the loss of the family home with all its memories, now comes the ultimate loss—the loss of their independence.

In a nursing home the oldster must become accustomed to someone else's routines and regulations. And changing habits for people set in their ways is not easy. (Think of the last time you tried to break your regular routine!) Depending upon their physical condition, many elderly who have always prided themselves on their own independence and self-reliance must now wait for someone else to take care of their most intimate needs.

Put yourself into your parent's situation for a time and sincerely try to imagine how you would feel. To do so often results in far more compassion, patience and understanding. When you are tempted to rush through the move to a nursing home because you are smarting from your own painful emotions or because you want to "get it over with," don't fail to consider the feelings of your loved one. Remember that the move is often a far more traumatic process for the oldster. Your parent needs all the love, compassion and encouragement you can possibly give. Verbalize that love and assure your parent that he or she is not being "put away to be forgotten." Openly discuss the fears and apprehensions you both may have. Moving into an extended care facility does not have to mean the end of a close, loving relationship.

Making the Move

Before your parent is admitted into the nursing home, find out from the director or administrator what personal items to bring. Most facilities require that all personal belongings be clearly marked with your parent's name. A laundry marking pen serves well for marking robes, bed jackets and house shoes.

Frequently my mother's robes disappeared, so I finally made labels by cutting white cotton fabric strips to sew onto her robe near the hem. I used a black felt tip pen to letter her name in one-inch letters on each label.

Unless prohibited, bring a number of familiar objects such as a plant, pictures, a favorite pillow and your parent's own Bible to add a touch of home to the new surroundings. We brought a small bulletin board that we were permitted to attach to the wall next to Mom's bed. On it we displayed cards or family photos. Her favorite seemed to be the school pictures of her grandchildren.

Each facility has its own admission procedures and methods of welcoming the newcomer and making him or her feel at home. Some nursing homes encourage a family member to stay for the first meal. Others assign a trained staff member to help the new resident become acquainted with the environment. Many facilities encourage relatives to devote a great deal of time visiting, even when a staff member is available. Other nursing homes do little to reach out to the newcomer, preferring to have family and relatives stay in the background following admission until the patient has adjusted and settled into the new environment.

Talk to the director and discover what the rules are. Open communication with the staff will avoid getting off on the wrong foot in this new three-way arrangement of care involving staff, loved one and family.

Parent's Adjustment

Many families are surprised and frequently frustrated to find their loved one does not immediately adjust to living in a nursing home. While it is very difficult to observe the slow and sometimes painful adjustment process demonstrated by some elderly, the family needs to be patient. Experts in the field report that it takes some new residents in a nursing home up to six months to adjust. That is a difficult time for the family. We all would like to see a quick, easy adjustment—an adjustment that would erase some of the mixed emotions faced by the family when placing a loved one into such a facility. Of course, some elderly who have been living alone and were very lonely adjust very quickly to having other residents and a helpful staff available. The "easy adjusters" often display an increase in appetite and are quick to respond to the activities provided by the staff. Other new residents become rather complacent and respond with a passive acceptance concerning the move.

If your loved one does not adjust as easily as you expected, don't be too quick to blame yourself, panic or immediately begin looking for a new facility. Moving your parent to another nursing home may not be the answer; in some cases it may create even greater stress and problems. If, however, there are obvious indications of abuse and/or neglect, seek help immediately from professionals like the Ombudsman program. In the case of abuse or neglect a move should seriously be considered.

During an ordinary adjustment period, continue to patiently encourage, support and pray with and for your parent. That is not to say that you are to ignore complaints your parent makes about neglect, rudeness from the staff or any other problems. Be alert to the quality of care received. Listen sympathetically and investigate all legitimate grievances. Talk to the nursing supervisor or home administrator about the complaint. Your investigation will demonstrate to the staff that you intend to be a concerned supporter of your parent. It will also reassure your loved one that you are deeply concerned for his or her welfare, and your concern will help to dismiss the fear of abandonment.

In all fairness to nursing home staff, the nurses, aides, orderlies and therapists are only human. They cannot perform miracles for the gravely ill any more than an acute care hospital can. Many staff members are kind, conscientious and sincerely concerned about the elderly in their care. Of course, there are some who are indifferent, lazy and sloppy—persons who should not even be on staff—but they are usually the exception.

In the eight years my mother was confined to an extended care facility I discovered that feelings of mutual respect between family and staff are vitally important. When that respect was evident it was much easier to feel we were a team working together for my mother's best welfare. Now before you say, "You haven't seen the nursing home where my parent is!" let me assure you that we, too, had to deal with inefficient, lazy, hostile aides. But when we did, because of the rapport and empathy between the director, the registered nurses and myself, my complaints appeared to carry more weight than if I had been an extremely critical or chronic complainer. The result? The careless, inefficient employee was reprimanded and, in some cases, dismissed. When I had complained about certain poor workers so much that I felt I dare not say more, I prayed fervently for their dismissal! Are you shocked? Don't be. I am sure several careless workers never knew why they lost their jobs, but I believe the Lord answered my prayers.

Family Adjustment

It may be surprising to discover that a move to a nursing home not only involves adjustment by a parent, but also means family adjustment. While your parent is in the process of adjusting, he or she may go through days of complaining and being very unhappy and depressed. If so, you may experience some of the "fall out" from these depressive emotions. Doubts may come and you may be tempted to question the wisdom of the decision you made. When this happens, don't give in to the doubts. Recognize that these feelings are part of *your* adjustment. You did what you had to do so that your parent could receive the twenty-four-hour-a-day skilled nursing care needed.

How well I remember my dark days of trying to adjust. As I became acquainted with other people who were visiting their parents in the facility, I found myself posing the identical question to each one: How long has your parent been here?

I knew, even as I asked that question, that secretly

Visits can become easier if motivated by love rather than a sense of duty. Be creative and try to think of ways to make the visit less tense and more pleasurable.

I wanted to hear a reponse indicating a short stay—a week, two weeks at most. My reasoning was that if I felt assured I could take Mom home in a few weeks, I could endure seeing her confined. The answer that stands out in my mind was the one from a daughter who patiently told me, "My mother has been here nine years."

Nine years! In my heart of hearts I screamed, "Oh, God, no! Please, God, not that long!"

My mother was in that facility for eight years. How good of our heavenly Father to keep us from knowing the future!

The Caregiver and the Nursing Home

Your role as a caregiver has not ended just because you have admitted your parent into a nursing home. It has only changed. Now you assume the roles of an encourager, a visitor, a mediator and an observer.

The Role of Encourager

As has already been indicated, you need to help your parent to adjust to the new environment. Introduce yourself and your parent to other residents. Encourage your parent to make new friends. If your parent is physically able, encourage participation in the activities program provided by the staff.

If permissible, take your parent out for an afternoon. The outing need not be elaborate. A trip to a local drive-in restaurant (check diet restrictions) or to a Dairy Queen can do wonders for a lonely nursing home resident.

Mom's favorite Saturday afternoon treat was for me to bring a thermos of hot Sanka from home and pick up some fresh Danish from a nearby bakery. An outing she thoroughly enjoyed many times during the week was an outdoor wheelchair ride after her evening meal. The hospital was located in a residential area, so I could push her wheelchair slowly up one street and down another as she admired the flowers and the birds. Sometimes we chatted, at other times she had a faraway smile as she quietly admired nature all around her.

Due to their physical condition our parents are primarily at the receiving end of having their needs met—a position that can easily destroy individual dignity. You can help to restore that dignity by occasionally bringing *small* treats for your parent to share with the staff and some of the residents. The treats will not only help to improve your parent's dignity and self-image, but the staff will usually accept the offer as a gesture of friendship—one that often results in greater interest in your parent. Now, I am not suggesting a bribe. Like most of us, members of a nursing home staff appreciate being known as caring individuals, rather than—in their case—uniforms under surveillance by the family.

The Role of Visitor

Many adult children have a difficult time visiting parents in nursing homes. For many, the visits stir up mixed emotions. The visits then become strained and, as a result, neglected. They excuse themselves for *not* visiting by saying, "We have nothing to say to one another," or "I can't stand to hear the complaints," or "My father is angry because he blames me for putting him there."

Visits can become easier if motivated by love rather than a sense of duty. Be creative and try to think of ways to make the visit less tense and more pleasurable. Your visits can help your parent stay in touch with family, the outside world and reality. The following suggestions will no doubt stimulate other ideas for you to make your visits more satisfying.

Make a tape recording of your family around the dinner table as each family member talks to Grandma or Grandpa. Bring your parent's pet for a short visit (if permissible). Suggest that you and your parent work together on a jigsaw puzzle (or another project). Conversation often is easier when hands are occupied and eye contact lessened. Offer to read to your parent and select items of interest from newspapers or magazines, read favorite Bible passages or a chapter from a Christian book. Bring a recording of some favorite hymns. Give your mother a manicure and hand massage as you talk. Offer to write a letter for your parent—this often results in incoming mail. Dig out the family photo album and relive old memories together. Join your parent in the activities provided by the nursing home.

For one of Mom's birthdays I brought a large angel food birthday cake for her to share with the staff and her roommates. News of the birthday bash spread throughout the hallways and soon numerous residents dropped by. I felt like the little boy with his lunch of loaves and fish as I kept cutting cake for the visitors, but we had enough for all.

Bring a grandchild or great-grandchild for a short visit. Be sure to prepare the child by saying something like, "Grandma will be so happy to see you she may cry, but that's okay." When you visit don't be afraid to touch, to hug and, above all, to listen—yes, even to the stories you have heard a million times before!

The Role of Mediator and Observer

Although nursing homes must pass rigid state inspection and abide by strict codes of operation, many families still experience problems concerning care of parents.

Problems can range from other patients wearing your parent's robes, to personal belongings disappearing, to unshaven men residents or those who obviously have not had hands or face washed after a meal. A very frustrating problem that frequently arises is when there is a consistent shortage of aides or orderlies, which means inadequate care for residents.

When these problems occur frequently you have a

duty and a right to talk with the nursing supervisor or the administrator. Make an appointment, if necessary, and discuss your area of concern. Be specific. Find out why personal hygiene, for example, is being neglected. If personal items are disappearing ask that aides be instructed to carefully check for labels bearing your parent's name on each item. If your parent is left in a wheelchair for hours without bathroom privileges, find out why. If a bedridden parent complains of being scolded for soiling the bed or asking for a bedpan, ask that the supervisor and/or administrator investigate, monitor the staff and report back to you.

Of course, to become unreasonably critical of the staff only leads to more problems, often involving the social service staff. But if, after you have met with the supervisory personnel, your parent receives no better care or you receive vague, unsatisfactory answers, you still have a recourse by contacting some of the following "watchdog" agencies.

Watchdog Groups

Negative publicity of neglect and, in some cases, abuse of nursing home residents has resulted in an increase in the number of community based watchdog organizations. The local Department of Health and Human Services, as well as your local Area Agency on Aging, are two groups to whom you may turn for guidance if you have a justifiable complaint concerning the rights or the care of your loved one. Another excellent watchdog group to whom you may report complaints is your local Long Term Care Ombudsman program, mentioned in chapter 10. Ombudsman has as its purpose "to receive, investigate and act on complaints" made by nursing home residents or their families.

At one time, I felt that voicing complaints about my mother's care could result in the staff retaliating against Mom, who was completely helpless. In reality, experts indicate that a resident whose family is alert and willing to confront and discuss a problem usually receives better care. Supervisory personnel are sometimes unaware of a problem; if the resident or the family fails to report the incident because of fear, a bad situation often rapidly becomes worse.

At the beginning of this chapter I indicated that we made a poor choice of nursing homes for my mother when we moved her from an acute care hospital. When we discovered that Mom was being inadequately cared for and was being verbally abused, we were heartsick. Unaware of any other recourse I immediately began to look for another facility. Despite the fact that Mom had only been in that convalescent hospital a couple of weeks, we—in desperation and rather naively—moved her to another facility.

At the time she was still receiving Medicare assistance, an extension from the acute care hospital, so we immediately received a letter asking us to explain the move. In my written reply I listed more than twelve incidents of verbal abuse and mistreatment, of neglect and inappropriate medication, all of which I had personally witnessed. In response I received a most gracious letter from the Department of Health and Human Service thanking me for the information. I was told an investigation was being made and that the facility was already under surveillance.

From experience I know that families and residents may rest assured that complaints are handled in confidence and without fear of reprisal.

To Tell or Not to Tell

Family members often become very uneasy when they begin to notice evidence that an elderly person is coming to the end of life and is "living on borrowed time."

The question uppermost in the hearts and minds of adult children is: Should the elderly be told that he or she is dying? Medical opinions vary. Many nurses with whom I have spoken indicate that most people, especially the elderly, are well aware that death is near. Some want to talk about it, while others do not. I was told by several medical professionals that the family need not force the subject. If the dying person questions the family, then of course, honesty demands that the truth not be withheld. In the heart and mind of the dying person there may be something he or she needs to say or have taken care of. Silence or evading the truth often leads to greater worry by some patients as they interpret their condition as being worse than it is.

Furthermore, how can anyone be denied the right to prepare for death? Once the truth is known, the person can work through whatever feelings necessary. This does not mean, however, that once the truth is out you need to keep referring to your parent's condition. Neither do you need to go into great detail. Allow the doctor to decide how much detail is necessary in answering questions and still provide peace of mind to your parent.

Prolonging Life

Modern society is divided about the issue of using heroic methods to keep up the medical fight for life when all hope for the individual's survival is gone. I do not advocate nor do I believe in euthanasia. I feel the ramifications of euthanasia can be more dangerous even than abortion. However, I do feel strongly that every individual has the right to choose not to be subjected to the pain and distress of being kept alive by means of machines and other instruments when all hope is gone.

It is very important that adult children discuss the issue of prolonging life with their parents long before the death crisis and while the parent is still of sound mind. Children need to make *absolutely sure* they understand the desires of their parents concerning this vital issue.

Several years before my mother's illness and surgery she read a news account of an elderly person who had been rushed to an acute care hospital several times and placed on life sustaining machines. The account disturbed Mom greatly. After reading the article aloud to me she said, "Please, don't ever let them do that to me!" The final outcome of that incident was that Mom made her wishes very clear to me and to my brothers. She wanted no part in heroic efforts for her life. She insisted that she firmly believed she would meet her Lord and Savior at death and she wanted no one to detain her. Several years later when the time came for that decision, while it was still very difficult for us, it was easier because we knew we were fulfilling her desires. Fortunately, at the time my mother died, no decision involving heroic methods was needed.

I was so thankful that my mother's doctor sat down with me and carefully defined in layman's language what the term "heroic methods" meant. I understood that it does not mean rejection of medical care. The patient, the doctor explained, would always be made as comfortable and free of pain as possible. But my mother's treatment would not include intubation (ask your doctor for an explanation) or being placed on instruments to keep her breathing indefinitely.

You and your parents need to discuss with the doctor what is meant by heroic methods, because I cannot begin to define the methods for you. Medical techniques are changing so rapidly, some methods

Death is as much a part of life as is birth....Each individual has only one father or mother to lose, and when a parent dies, some part of the child dies also.

that at one time might have been considered to be life saving techniques are now no longer considered such.

If it is your parents' wish to avoid futile treatment when they become terminally ill, it is well for them to meet with their lawyer and make out living wills, if they have not already done so. You and your parents need to discuss the terms of the wills with their physician so that all concerned are aware of those terms. Your parents may also wish to give copies of their living wills to other close members of the family.

The decision for using a living will is a very individual, personal matter. It is a choice that must not be made by anyone other than the individual whose life is involved. The decision must rest with the person who faces death.

The Final Curtain

King Solomon, a man noted for his wisdom, once said, "There is a time for everything, and a season for every activity under heaven: a time to be born and a time to die."[1] Death is as much a part of life as is birth. Nevertheless, the issues of death and dying and how to react to those issues are never easy. Despite their age we never seem quite ready for the final crisis of the death of a parent. Each individual has only one father or mother to lose, and when a parent dies, some part of the child dies also.

Thanks to author Elizabeth Kübler-Ross and her well known book, *On Death and Dying,* the public has become familiar with the various stages persons go through who face death, namely: denial, anger, bargaining, depression and, finally, acceptance. Of course, people often move back and forth between these stages, and many experience several stages at the same time. I believe my mother did.

While Kübler-Ross's work has been helpful, many people still find it difficult to know how to respond to a parent who hints at a desire to talk about death by making such comments as, "After I'm gone..." or "When I am no longer here, I want you to...." Some adult children say they feel nervous and uneasy when a parent begins to "talk like that," so the children try to change the subject. Perhaps a kinder response —although admittedly more difficult—is to permit your parent to continue. Many elderly are eager to discuss their feelings and are often frustrated and saddened because they are not permitted to do so. A number of adult children, in speaking of their parents' deaths, have admitted their deep regret for not having talked more freely with their parents while they still had the chance.

Some elderly want time before the final crisis to exchange ideas about their conditions and to be assured that all is well between parent and children. That time of sharing can become a time for any needed forgiveness or reconciliation, as well as financial instructions and expressions of deep love.

My family members are firm believers in life after death. We believe the promise of the Bible that our Lord has prepared a place for us,[2] and we claim the promise of Christ who said, "I am the resurrection, and the life; he who believes in Me shall live even if he dies."[3] My mother talked freely about going to be with the Lord and seeing Dad and all of the loved ones who had gone on before. This was not morbid at all, but an expression of a deep, confident belief of what was in store for her. She described it as "going home."

People differ. The cue for discussion should come from the dying person. Your parent *may not* want to discuss death, and that is his or her right.

While death is an enemy, for the Christian believer there is victory over this enemy because we have the assurance that the Lord Jesus Christ conquered death. The believer can say with confidence, "Death has been swallowed up in victory. Where, O death, is your victory? Where, O death, is your sting?"[4] Our hope is the promise of our Lord when He said, "Whoever lives and believes in me will never die."[5] To depart from this life is to be with our Lord forevermore.

211

Moving into a Nursing Home

Notes

1. Ecclesiastes 3:1-2.
2. John 14:1-3.
3. John 11:25, *NASB*.
4. 1 Corinthians 15:54-55.
5. John 11:26.

Chapter Twelve
Power to Cope!

As I indicated at the beginning of this book, my goal in writing has been to share some of the answers I discovered to the baffling questions adult children face when caring for their aging parents. I trust you have found some answers, but you no doubt have discovered, even as I have, that some questions have no easy, simple answers. And to some questions there are *no* answers at all!

There is one additional question I have been asked many times, but one which I have not yet answered. Time and again, adult children have asked, "How did *you* cope when your mother was in a hospital for eight years?"

No, this was not a note of admiration for any outstanding abilities I may have displayed. The hidden message was a query that seemed to ask: Did you find a key or a clue that could help me make life easier for my parent and myself as we face these times?

The answer to that question is that the only way I managed to endure while my mother was confined to a convalescent hospital was my faith in the living God and the strength and guidance I received from His

Word. In fact, that is another very important reason I had for writing this book—to express my gratitude to God by telling you what He did for me. To paraphrase that old song made famous by Stewart Hamlin years ago: What God has done for me, He will do for you. Woven throughout the eight years of my mother's hospital stay and my emotional upheavals and heartaches is a bright, strong thread of the enduring faithfulness of our loving heavenly Father.

As Thy Day

One of the many advantages of growing up in a Christian home, as I did, is that you are usually exposed to Scripture most of your life. You hear it daily, you read it and you memorize it. When a crisis occurs it is not surprising that a Bible verse or promise comes to mind and it may well be a Scripture you have not thought about for years. A verse I had learned sometime during my earlier years came to me at a time I least expected it, but it came just when I really needed it.

It was a cold, dark October morning during a period of my life when it seemed that everything that could go wrong, did. My mother, who shared my home at that time, was very ill. Surgery was scheduled for her, but with little hope of survival. Our washer had broken down and my work load at the office was extremely heavy, with countless deadlines just around the corner. Mom's doctor decided that, due to her age and weakened condition, he wanted to "build her up at home for a month" before surgery in an attempt to improve her prognosis. I wanted the best for my mother, despite the fact that my work load at home would increase during the time she gained strength for surgery.

214

Long before dawn that October morning, while Mom still slept, I rushed to the Laundromat with a huge load of laundry. Every moment of the morning was carefully planned. I would do the washing, hurry home and prepare breakfast for Mom, do a quick cleanup and still get to the office on time. I was fortunate to be the only occupant in the Laundromat at that hour, so I could use as many washers as I needed. Moments before my laundry was ready for the dryers, a lady rushed in and, to my amazement, deposited coins into most of the dryers! Then she went out to her parked van and brought in several baskets of wet laundry, which she promptly tossed into the dryers.

I couldn't believe my eyes! So much for my well-planned schedule. I had no choice but to wait for some of the dryers. Of course, that should not have been a major crisis, but since I was already tired and tense from the pressures at home, it was the last straw for me. I dissolved into tears. Staring out into the darkness, waves of self-pity swept over me. In my heart I wailed, "Lord I can't take anymore! This is too much!" Then into my mind flashed these words: "As thy days, so shall thy strength be."[1]

I wish I could say I snapped right out of my depression, but I didn't. By the time the dryers were free for me to use, however, I had begun to feel a little less frustrated. A deep sense of peace began to settle over me, despite the fact that my schedule, which I felt was already hectic, had just worsened to impossible. During the day I managed to snatch a few moments to check my concordance to find the verse that had continued to run through my mind throughout the busy hours. While I did not realize it that day as I highlighted God's promise in my Bible, I was to refer to that verse many times within the next eight years. I had to believe God's promise. It was a matter of faith—like a lifesaver tossed into my dark sea of fear and frustration.

Tenaciously I hung on to God's promise for strength as my mother went through surgery, as well as the month immediately following her surgery. For four weeks I froze each time the phone rang for fear the call would bring bad news. Despite my fears, guilt and failures, as each new day dawned the Lord was faithful to His promise. He provided the necessary strength and wisdom to solve our problems and to take us through those difficult hours.

Although my mother improved enough to be transferred to a convalescent hospital, the doctor's prognosis was still that my mother was living on limited time. As the days turned into weeks and the weeks into months, problems arose that seemed too big to solve, and we tried to give our worries over to God—although not always very successfully. Looking back it is interesting to see how some of the things I worried about never became a reality. My mother would have labeled those worries "borrowed trouble," and that evaluation would have been correct, as is evident from the following incident.

The First Mother's Day

A well-known fact is that Christmas holidays are usually very difficult for people experiencing serious emotional and/or personal problems. I discovered that Christmas is not the only holiday that can be difficult.

It was a week before Mother's Day. One evening as the nurses and I chatted someone commented, "Mother's Day here at the hospital is always a big day.

We go all out. We have open house with a tea for the families."

No one could deny the consideration and concern that motivated the celebration. But all week as I heard the staff plan and watched them decorate for the occasion, my spirits dropped. By the end of the week I felt very depressed. My mother was the typical old-fashioned mother who devoted her life to her home and family. Never had she been away from her children on Mother's Day. With the birth of grandchildren the day had become even more special for Mom, as children and grandchildren helped her celebrate her special day. If only we could take her to one of our homes for the day, but she was not well enough.

Within a few days I had convinced myself that Mother's Day that year would be a sad, morbid day. I worried that Mom would be wrapped in homesickness and loneliness. What else could we expect on this, her first Mother's Day in a hospital? Since she wasn't well enough to have everyone come to see her in one afternoon, I encouraged my brothers to be with their own wives and families, and I would visit Mom.

The day before Mother's Day I went to see Mom and found her in a deep, unnatural sleep, and very sluggish. Alarmed, I immediately questioned the charge nurse. "Your mother has had some sort of a small vascular disturbance," said the nurse. "We can't really explain it, but the doctor has been in to see her. This often happens to patients who are your mother's age and in her condition. Don't worry, we're watching her very closely."

On Mother's Day I went to the hospital feeling sad and wondering how to cheer Mom. She was asleep. I sat beside her bed all afternoon, but Mom slept right through the day. The nurses were in and out of her room, assuring me that Mom was in no pain. Somehow the day I had dreaded so very much was not as bad as I had expected. My mother was spared the feeling of loneliness, even though she was away from her family. By Monday she was quite alert and pretty much herself again. She was completely unaware that she had missed Mother's Day and was happy to see me when I came in for my daily visit. How grateful I was that she had been spared any additional heartache!

The Power of the Word

Weeks and months of Mom's hospital stay turned into years. My mother's physical condition continued to keep us on an emotional roller coast ride as she hit frightening physical lows when I feared we had reached the end. After each low she experienced improvement, and we were relieved and grateful for the lack of suffering. The medical staff labeled many of these lows as "vascular disturbances"—no doubt due to lack of a better term in layman's language. The doctor explained that the disturbances often caused patients to become giddy, depressed, or very angry and irritable. I felt my mother went through all of these stages at various times throughout the years.

One evening when I came to visit she was especially restless and irritable. Of course, I realized she was not responsible, but I felt so helpless! Everything I or anyone else *did* was wrong. And everything I *said* irritated her. In desperation I began reading to her from the *Living Bible*. Almost immediately Mom stopped tossing and scolding. As I flipped through the Psalms at random, I was thrilled that the old familiar message had hit a responsive chord and brought peace.

Then I came to Psalm 23:4: "Even when walking through the dark valley of death..." I increased my reading speed because I didn't want to set her off by thinking I had intentionally chosen a passage that spoke about death.

"What did that say?" asked Mom. "Read it again—and slowly, please!"

What a delight to see the power of the Word of God!...Not only did God's Word frequently calm my mother; I, too, learned to lean heavily upon God's promises.

I did read it again. Mom knew the twenty-third Psalm well. She had learned it in the German language as a child. It was one of the first psalms she had taught us to say when we were young. Now the familiar words in a modern paraphrase spoke to her and met a special need. Together we quoted bits of the psalm in German. I was surprised how many German phrases came back to my rusty mind, and Mom was thrilled to hear them. Memories drifted through her mind and brought a smile as she said contentedly, "That's right. He is right here with me."

What a delight to see the power of the Word of God! Soon Mom dropped off into a peaceful sleep, and I went home relieved.

Not only did God's Word frequently calm my mother; I, too, learned to lean heavily upon God's promises. Mother had been confined in the hospital for five years when she again became very ill. I stayed at the hospital that night until the nurse sent me home. I was hesitant about leaving because I wasn't at all sure Mom would make it through the night.

Worry, fear and heartache no doubt colored my attitude. I felt angry that Mom had to suffer so long. As I drove home I cried and tried to pray. Sadly, my prayer was more of a list of complaints than a real prayer. How grateful I am for the mercy and compassion of our God who doesn't give up on us! One by one I listed my concerns for my mother's welfare—complaints that centered primarily around what I felt to be an inadequate staff of nurses on duty that night.

Then it was as though the Lord spoke to me. Let me be quick to assure you I did not hear an audible voice in the car that night, but these thoughts came to mind: "Remember, even when walking through the dark valley...*I* will be close beside her, guarding and guiding all the way. It doesn't really matter *who* is with her. *I will be there!*" And once again I had to commit my mother into His hands.

A Difficult Move

When Mom had been in the hospital for almost seven years, the publishing company for whom I have worked for many years moved to Ventura, sixty miles from Glendale where Mom was hospitalized. Months before our office moved, my brothers and I tried to find a hospital in the Ventura area so that we could move my mother. All hospitals there were filled. We placed our name on the waiting list at seven facilities.

Confidently, I prayed and waited upon the Lord to provide a bed for my mother. When our search for an extended care facility in Ventura failed, the question *Why?* became a long playing record in my mind. Why did Mom have to lie in a hospital for so many years? She had always prayed that the Lord would spare her from extended care. Why did she have to be deprived of the one bright spot in her day—my daily visit?

Over and over I read such promises as "in quietness and trust is your strength" and "the Lord longs to be gracious to you; he rises to show you compassion. For the Lord is a God of justice. Blessed are all who wait for him!"[2] And again: "How great is your goodness to those who publicly declare that you will rescue them."[3] I assured friends who asked about my plans for my mother that I was confident the Lord would provide a place for her in or near Ventura. But nothing opened up. Had God forgotten us now, after supplying our needs so faithfully all these years? Deep down in my heart I knew that was not the answer, for the Lord was so gracious in working out all the details of moving the office and finding a new home for me. At times I felt I had to run to keep up with the many blessings He so graciously showered upon me. Only my prayers to move Mom went unanswered.

I felt so sorry for my mother. By this time she was unable to speak to make her requests known to the nurses. She was completely helpless, unable to feed herself or even turn over in bed. I worried about the care she would receive, as well as her loneliness when I was unable to visit her daily. The hardest part was that I did not know whether she understood why I only visited on weekends, rather than daily as in the past. I didn't want her to feel abandoned in her help-lessness. But no matter how much we prayed about the matter, the heavens appeared to be made of brass. So it was a dark day, indeed, when I moved to Ventu-ra, leaving Mom in a hospital so far from me.

For almost a year and a half after I moved to Ventu-ra, I drove to Glendale and spent each weekend with Mom. Through all that time I knew the Lord was the One who supplied the daily strength for what I had to do. I also knew that when the time was right the Lord would either open a hospital room for Mom in Ventura or He would take her home to be with Him. In the meantime I tried to trust and wait upon Him.

Yes, those were difficult days. Looking back, I would not like to go through that time again, but nei-ther would I take anything for the experience. Why? Because despite the heartaches involved with my mother's disability, the Lord was good and the Bible became very precious to me. At the darkest hours when days of fear and worry seemed to overwhelm me and I felt lonely and forgotten, a most appropriate message would almost seem to leap off the pages of my Bible, despite the fact that I didn't understand the why of my situation: "Do not fear...I have called you by name; you are Mine! When you pass through the waters, I will be with you; and through the rivers, they will not overflow you. When you walk through the fire, you will not be scorched...For I am the Lord your God, the Holy One...your Saviour."[4] Promise after pre-cious promise became my source of strength. I was not alone, for He was with me, and with that knowledge I was able to take life one day at a time.

God Is Faithful

Early one morning my phone rang. Instinctively, I knew it was the hospital. Once again I was told that my mother was gravely ill. As I rushed around preparing to leave for Glendale, I realized that it was exactly eight years to the day since my mother had the initial attack that had resulted in her needed surgery.

I spent the weekend at Mom's bedside. When she improved slightly the doctor felt I could safely return to work. It was a difficult decision. I knew my work was piling up on my desk in Ventura, but my mother was still quite ill. With the doctor's encouragement I finally decided to dash back to the office for a day, take care of the most pressing jobs, then return to Glendale. My employer was most gracious and urged me to take as much time off as necessary.

All went as planned—the work was completed and I would go to Glendale Thursday morning. At eleven o'clock on Wednesday night, however, I received a call indicating that Mom's condition had worsened. The doctor wanted to move her to an acute care hospital immediately.

My heart jumped into my throat. I wanted Mom to be made as comfortable as possible, but an acute care hospital could mean heroics and life support machines. She had definitely made me promise not to permit heroics. I knew she would be frightened and I wanted to be with her. Tossing my bag into the car I left for Glendale. I had no idea which hospital had been chosen. As I sped down the freeway I tried to pray, only to realize I didn't know what to pray for! All I could say was, "However you work this out, Lord, is okay. Please don't let her suffer. Please take control—this is beyond me!" And He did.

It was midnight when I arrived at the convalescent hospital in Glendale. There I was told no bed was available in an acute care hospital, so Mom would not be moved. I could only take that news as God's answer to my prayer. When I went into my mother's room she was sleeping quietly.

My mother lingered throughout the day. I had, of course, been in contact with my brothers, but the doctor felt they would not need to come to the hospital just yet. It was a rough day as I stayed with my mother, but the Lord graciously gave me a calm and an inner peace beyond human description.

Much to my relief, Mrs. MacArthur, my favorite R.N., was on duty caring for my mother all day. In fact, that nurse came back for the night shift—which meant she was doing double duty! I will always be deeply grateful to her for her love and compassion.

By 10:30 Thursday night it was obvious that the Lord's perfect timing had almost arrived. I put in telephone calls to my brothers. As I sat beside Mom's bed waiting for them to arrive, my mind went back over the past eight years. How many times we'd sat at Mom's bedside praying, and how many times the Lord had comforted us—as well as Mom—and supplied our every need. Promise after promise, which we'd shared together from the Word, came to mind. I continued praying that my brothers would not run into heavy traffic, and that they would arrive in time. I knew how much they wanted to be there; besides, I didn't really want to be alone when Mom slipped away. My feelings were mixed. I didn't want it to happen, even though I knew she had everything to gain and nothing to lose.

The familiar words from the twenty-third Psalm, which my mother had loved so much, came to mind: "Even when walking through the valley..." The words were as clear as if someone had spoken them, although there was no audible voice. "You [God] are

---

In a short time Mom would see her Savior face-to-face!...While nothing in the hospital room changed...that room became a sacred sanctuary.

---

close beside me, guarding, guiding all the way." I was well aware that my mother was very close to walking *through* that valley of death.

Suddenly, I realized this was not a time to be frightened. This was a most sacred moment. At any second the Creator of the Universe, my Savior and Lord, would be ushering my mother into His presence. I could almost hear the rustle of angels' wings! Despite the tears that trickled down my cheeks, I felt a bit like Moses of old when God told him, "Take off your sandals, for the place where you are standing is holy ground."[5] In a short time my mother would see her Savior face-to-face! Soon she would be in the presence of the One whom she had served so faithfully all her life. While nothing in the hospital room had changed—no lights, voices or other phenomena—that room became a sacred sanctuary where I felt the very presence of the Lord.

My brothers arrived in ample time. Shortly after midnight our quiet, shy little mother slipped peacefully away from us into the presence of her Lord. While there were tears, we also experienced a deep reassurance of our faith, indicating that being absent from the body, she was now present with the Lord. She had been granted her heart's desire—she was free at last.

As my brothers and I walked out of the hospital in the wee hours of the morning, the words of another promise the Lord had given me eight years earlier flashed through my mind: "As thy days, so shall thy strength be." Those eight years were the most difficult I have ever experienced, but God had truly been faithful in keeping His promise. There was always enough strength and encouragement for each day.

If you, as a caregiver, are going through some difficult, traumatic days, take heart. There is life after caregiving! Look to the Lord for the strength to take you through the difficult days. He is faithful to His promises—take it from someone who knows from experience.

Notes

1. Deuteronomy 33:25, *KJV*.
2. Isaiah 30:15,18.
3. Psalm 31:19, *TLB*.
4. Isaiah 43:1-3, *NASB*.
5. Exodus 3:5.

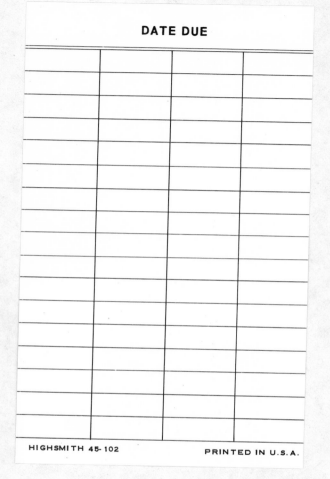

DATE DUE

HIGHSMITH 45-102   PRINTED IN U.S.A.